101 Elsie St

DOMINIC ALBANESE

ALSO BY DOMINIC ALBANESE

Notebook Poems
Bastards Had the Whole Hill Mined
Iconic Whispers
Then-n-Now
Love Is Not Just a Word (with Seb Doubinsky)
Only the River Knows
The Wizard & the Wrench (with Ambika Devi)
Boardwalk Dreams
Midway Moves
Disconnected Memories
By Some Happenstance
Poets & Jugglers
Dear Miss B
Prepare for World Flip-Out

101 Elsie St

DOMINIC ALBANESE

Poetic Justice Books

Copyright ©2023 Dominic Albanese

book design and layout: SpiNDec, DeLand, FL
cover design: Kris Haggblom

All rights reserved.

No part of this book may be used or reproduced in any manner whatsoever without written permission except in the case of brief quotations embodied in critical articles and reviews. Members of educational institutions and organizations wishing to photocopy any of the work for classroom use, or authors, artists and publishers who would like to obtain permission for any material in the work, should contact the publisher.

Published by Poetic Justice Books
DeLand, Florida
email: poeticjusticebna@gmail.com

ISBN: 978-1-950433-66-7 (hardcover)
       978-1-950433-67-4 (paperback)
       978-1-950433-91-9 (e-book)

10 9 8 7 6 5 4 3 2 1

Ten years? Really? Only ten years? I feel like I've known Dominic for a lifetime, like he's always been there. The comfortable way of settling in to a conversation, the quick shorthand of comfortable friendships.

101 Elsie St is the sixth book I've worked on with Dominic, the second non-poetry one. Though to call anything by Dominic "non-poetry" is to do it a disservice. All his work is an intimate space art performed just for you, a (most definitely not) whispered secret. Dinner and coffee fireside. Dominic has an uncanny ability to sneak in and set up camp in your mind, the stories all familiar yet totally new. He follows the path of the traditional storyteller without being anywhere near traditional.

I have heard many of the tales of *Elsie Street* in a kaleidoscope of iterations over those ten years, and yet this surreal road trip veering wildly from psychedelic nightmare to idyllic dream is an utterly new experience. And that, of course, is the job of storyteller – hold the interest, make them hold their breath. Every time Dominic spills ink, the world learns something about itself and we are all the better for it.

- Kris Haggblom, Poetic Justice Books

FOR ALL WE HAVE BEEN AND WILL BE
I offer this up with both prayers and salutations
for those here and those gone

Contents

Nobody Wants To Know Him They Can See He Is Just A Fool – 1

Broken Window Empty Hallway – 9

And We Both Know What Love Can Bring – 13

Many A Tear Has To Fall, But It's All A Game – 53

Out Of The Dark I Hear Them Calling
(Going To Prison Saved My Life) – 61

What A Long Strange Trip It's Been – 69

It's Not Something You Get Over – 75

But It's Something You Get Through – 83

Walking My Baby Back Home – 95

They Asked Me How I Knew – 103

All The Places And Things – 113

Gone To Rest – 127

But I'm Leaving Once Again – 129

All Things Must End – 137

*...And I'm going to take a liberty here, like in regard to "O what hard luck stories they all hand me," and did you ever read the Ukrainian poets? Hah! Before this war, **90%** of America did not even know where or what Ukrainian was. I think being since even when I was like 8 years old an the RED MENACE was gonna blow me out from under my desk, but long as I was not play wit my weenie I would get to meet Jesus. (or some shit)....inspired I am when told by my teacher, "You do write really well." What I see, what I feel is the empty page is that place to get lost in; it really is...emotions and happenstance...yeah...we all, and to me you very clearly see an know how things could be way better an way less o you know HATE FEAR ANGER RAGE but mostly just bullshit to cover up the fact the ones who are supposed to be running things, do not even have a clue about what really is going on or even less of what to do. THE POSTURE an pose...empty suits talking points an yeah long as the lobby money flows....o shit any how....since all my visits an my social ramble are over ....an they are I am make it now a VOW to get up, stop looking at what who said what or how many notify or likes I got..an get them books FUCKING DONE....this one here yeah, it is still a struggle for me to write good grammar an punctuate even at high school level I DON'T GIVE A Toss.....I*

gonna do it, an with some help from Kris an Corina make it be a bit more LEGIBLE but not loose my voice or style to just be, salable..or like that....far as the rest goes....I NEVER took all that duck an cover serious I really did not....being in Vietnam did teach me there is not a bottom nope just deeper holes the POWER mad are willing to go..to either gain more power more money or some how convince them self MURDER IS NOT MURDER if you do it with the approval of congress or some shit....as of this week, an the ever changing stories about...Putin Biden Trump shit Ali Babba for that matter.. IF WE DO JUST EVAPORATE in some radioactive cloud...I don't wanna be regret the time I did not work an do what I have been able to do O Carol, I am so glad you saw this house an see what I am blessed with long as I can keep up with the bills, an by the month, now with doing the pool my self an not spend a dime on cigars....I think I can...funny thing is....one my friends, sent me a gift card for dog food all well THANK YOU for send that to me...I am gonna do 101 ELSIE ST as stories and memories. William Boyal said DEAR MISS B was as good as anything he has read in years time an place in Brooklyn, that just stoke my fire.

101 Elsie St

DOMINIC ALBANESE

NOBODY WANTS TO KNOW HIM THEY CAN SEE HE IS JUST A FOOL

Even if this book does bounce around here and there. Back way back, to Cure of Ar's Catholic school. I remember today about Mother Superior Sister Jean Roseair, on first name basis with my dad. 4th and 5th grade were total torture on me, Dominic with the Dominican sisters, who for the most part seem to have a real hard case on boys, and all the time talk about *impure* thoughts, ya wag ya weenie ya going to hell...

Move through the holes and keep moving.

I have a choice: a ticket in the Lower Forty-Eight, or an extra $650 added to what the Army calls my mustering-out payment. I have in my kit bag about $6000, a few ounces of Cambodian Red Weed, a .45 pistol, two sets of civilian clothes, and a sale brochure for Harley motorcycles. March of 1966. I am out of the Army, released in Oakland, California. Only the one thing I want out is me, I want out of this uniform, out of these boots.

I met another guy in Oakland who was also getting out. He lived in San Francisco, and his brother was coming to pick him up. I asked if I could get a ride there, and they said they were glad to take me. They dropped me downtown. I checked into a hotel on Jones Street in my full-dress uniform, then asked the bellhop where to buy some shoes. He pointed out the door and said, "'Bout a block up left is a shoe store and a men's clothing store."

I found the store and bought a pair of high-top sneakers, a pair of work boots, a soft bag, a jacket and some socks. All I had were olive drab Army socks, so the socks I bought were white.

I go to eat at this place and the guy who runs it sees me in uniform and says, "On the house, soldier. On the house." In spite of the fact that even that early into the war, the anti-war sentiment in Frisco was pretty heated. I ate and had two glasses of some fancy wine. On the house. I went back to the hotel and passed out.

Check-out time the next day was at 11AM. I paid for another night, then got a cab to Oakland. In Oakland I bought a 600-miles-on-it '65 Harley Sportster, which cost around $1000 less than the '66 model. The sales manager asked me where I was from and if I had someone to service the bike. I told him, "I'm just back from Vietnam, and I'm gonna ride this bike to New York City."

He motioned for me to follow him into the back area where they were prepping the bike. He told the service manager to put some softer shocks on the back and replace the tires with a bit wider tread. He said the store was paying for it.

On the house. I stood there, and the sales guy cut me a hiball salute and said, "Welcome home, troop." I returned a salute and thanked him.

The service manager told me the upgrade was worth around three to five hundred dollars, and he also said he bet the sales manager was paying out of his own pocket because the dealership owner doesn't give away ice in the wintertime. Nice bike, black and silver, and they also put a bit wider fender on the front and adjusted the front brake with a stronger grip. I took the bike out along 14th Avenue, didn't push it at all, then turned back and picked up the paperwork. I drove the bike across the Bay Bridge back to San Francisco. I came off the freeway at the Embarcadero exit and drove up and down the docks that were full of trucks on the curb and forklifts in and out, loading all kinds of things being sent over to Asia.

Back at the hotel, I asked the bellhop where to find a motorcycle shop. He sent me to Fell Street, the Kosman specialty shop. I got my soft bag and rode over to the shop. I asked for a bracket to be made and mounted on the rear of the bike to hold the bag. I also needed a helmet. The mechanic, Bill Crosby, he was a good guy who would become a very close friend of mine, looked over the bike and said, "This is not a touring bike. Who put this set of tires on it?" I told him about the dealer in Oakland and he said, "Give me 'bout an hour and I'll dial this in a bit better. I'll mount that bag and when are you planning to leave?" I told him I was probably going to cruise round the Bay Area for a day and then I planned on taking the southern route because I bet some snow would still be on US 80. He pulled out an atlas created by the American Motorcycle Association and told me to have a seat and look over the routes laid out in the book. It goes without saying all I saw and thought about was Route 66. I plotted my path south and across Arizona, and the map of Texas looked to me like it was going to take not one but two or three weeks to cross. Oh boy, holes in the memory bank about that trip, but I did it. And the funny thing looking back is thinking about *Easy Rider*, and how I was anything but. I didn't have a driver's license and all I had for an ID was my military one. Knowing with all the pot and the pistol I had on me, it was best to just play it low and slow and not get pulled over.

In what would turn into a two-year back-and-forth across America, it began in San Francisco, touring around and then going up on Bernal Heights and stopping at Elsie St. At that time in '66 there lived in a house on Elsie St. a guy named Steve Raines, who was a master carpenter and artist and a bit of a ladies' man. I told him about seeing that house almost four years before, prior to Vietnam and all that, and he was moved and invited me in and we had a long talk. I met some of his friends, who later, as I got to engage and know people there, would become very close friends of mine. Like George and Gwen DuBois, who would a few years later name their son Dominic Leon DuBois, after me and Leon Russell. What a time that was. The backside of Bernal stretched to Dog Patch; unpaved, full of bikers, dope dealers and assorted hippy types and some hard ass working class longshoremen and a guy named Micheal O'Sullivan who would become one of my lifelong pals.

After about a month of couch camp, in and out of North Beach and some other districts there, I had met bikers, surfers, artists and, yeah, had a few love affairs. One of the women I love to this day, and I wager I have written at least five poems about her. Mary Ann, who could read your aura, know your heart and your soul. Once we were riding on my bike and stopped at Taylor and Pacific overlooking the Bay, a panorama unique to San Francisco. We had not even kissed, but she knew I was very attracted to her. We sat there a bit and she looked at me with her green eyes, deep into whoever or whatever I was at that time. "What have you done, where have you been? I see things that are dark and hidden in who I see as a bright and loving man." And she kissed me before I could kiss her, and then I asked her about our future. To this day I recall what she said, word for word: "Only love will clear up those dark things and it will take a long time, more time than I am willing to spend." We rode away from the panorama and stopped at a café. We talked a bit more, she kissed me again, got up and left, and I never saw her again.

    That made it time to go back to NYC, the long way. I really don't remember the trip down to US 5 or much at all about riding through Southern California, other than 1 through Big Sur, and down to where I connected to Arizona. That part lasted almost a month, and as funny as it sounds, in Flagstaff I was colder than I've ever been. I had to wrap a tarp over my clothes, and the wind on the bike bit into me.

    Down to Tucson is many pages unto itself. Names? Places? Well, one is the name Frank Gray, the name of a man who I knew from Okinawa. He was sitting in a Mexican food place. I walked in, and he nearly fell off his chair. "Monk San, can it really be you?" Yup, me all ragged-ass, dirty and windblown. His wife's brother owned the restaurant, and at the time her other brother was one of the biggest marijuana supply guys in Mexico. They lived down a little way in Oracle, on a ranch that looked to me like it must have at one time been for horses. There was a big barn that had hundreds of green or clear-wrap kilos, and Frank and his brother-in-law had a booming business, but of course it was very low key. In fact, if you know the movie *Blow*, it was Frank who supplied that guy in real life, and another guy who lived in Nebraska or somewhere bought a thousand or so kilos at a time. He offered them to me at forty dollars a kilo, and I could have as many as I thought I could sell and pay for them when I came back for more.

Well, there's no way to carry kilos on a motorcycle, and with my pistol and the bit I still had left from Asia, I was already a two-wheel jail sentence in the making. Frank told me to go see Billy Cheese, and I did. He had a combination junkyard-repair shop-small used lot. There was a gray '64 VW van there with a blown-up engine. Billy Cheese told me, "You fix it you can have it. Frank told me you saved his life." I said, "No he saved mine," and Billy replied, "I can only go by what he told me."

Billy Cheese let me use his shop and tools. I rebuilt the engine, and upgraded it with better cylinder heads, dual carbs and a way better oil cooling system. I asked him if I could leave my bike there. "As long as I can ride it when I want." Done deal. The van was tight and had a false floor that one of Billy's guys helped me install.

Back to Frank's and my first 100 kilo load, headed to NYC, and when I look back all these years later, I see it was how the times were then, how it was either an angel or pure dumb luck that I never got stopped or had even a burp in the van, all the way from Arizona to Coney Island, where I parked the van in back of the gas station I used to work at when I was fourteen years old.

Then my cousin hooked me up with Richie from the mafia who said he would give me $150 or $200 a kilo depending on how good it was. He bought the first hundred with a brown paper bag full of hundred-dollar bills.

More money than I'd ever seen in my life. And anyone reading this, if you think that was happenstance or just like I said dumb luck, it went on for two years, back and forth. I wore out the first van and got an even better one from Billy Cheese and paid him $3,000 for that one. I made enough money to get into Elsie Street, and have stupid money, and was really at the top of my game. Richie was this stocky guy with pretty good manners and dressed nice, but he had this way about him that you could tell he was not some one to trifle with. Did it stay that way? Yes, for about a year, until I tried cocaine, and that's how the next so many pages of fun and adventure and falling in love with the woman who would birth my only child came crashing down around me. These pages of people and places and things from that period… And then the wheels fell off.

Having just been in the Bay Area for a few months, in that mix of hippies, bikers, dope dealers, surfers, artists and all of that, Arizona—especially Tucson and its outlying areas—was something else. A bit more of Arizona and them days between good and bad times.

BROKEN WINDOW EMPTY HALLWAY

There was a shop in Tucson with twin brothers who were rebuilding a car for this woman who I would later get to know very well. The car was an early '60s Mercedes Benz 190 sedan. They converted it with a Ford pickup truck running gear, a 351 V-8, and a 4-speed manual transmission, with a very low first gear. They knew what Ford was all about but didn't know European cars at all. I was busy building a motor for my VW van but I did help them pull the old 6-cylinder Benz engine and transmission, and helped them weld in the new motor mounts and the sub-frame cradle for the new transmission. The only out-of-shop modification that had to be done was to build a drive shaft and yoke for the stock rear end. I had about a few thousand bucks left, and if I had to pay for the parts and upgrade to the van, it would have tapped me out.

All in all, it took about a month. I didn't meet the woman there but met her in NYC. Her name was Betsy, and later on she would be roommates with Aline Kominsky who would marry Robert Crumb. She didn't bring the car to NYC. She left it in Arizona, and when she moved to San Francisco she brought it there. As strange as this sounds, I would later work on and service that car from 1969 to about 1974 or so in San Francisco. The other thing is while in NYC she was involved with Ken Weaver of The Fugs, who was very close to the artist Spain Rodriguez who was lifelong my best friend. Mix-up, mashup of people, places and things. The Harley bike I left with Billy Cheese in Tucson. He would later supply me with another really outstanding Porsche 912 4-cylinder engine that I would put in another van. I traded him the bike for that motor and the body of the one I used the last few times crossing the country and the one I moved from NYC to Frisco in, and I never did go back to NYC except once in 1970 to show my dad my new baby daughter.

Here's one from those days in New York. I was sort of broke, and brother Tommy hooked me up with Richie from the Mafia. I had about eight or nine kilos left, and Richie comes by and pays me for a load I had not been paid for. He did the right thing.

I think also how in Vietnam you're never more alive than when you get shot at and shoot back, and you ducked another scary deal, almost like Uncle Tony and his fake foot. How I can remember Uncle Tony at 4 years old? But I do. Never thinking about death. Just a mostly scared kid. I don't think like that at all now; that is another part of my shunted shorted internal wire harness. I did think about death a lot. Meantime, between going out on patrol, put on them boots, get on that chopper and be the jazz, the well shit ain't kill me yet, let's just see how far this can all go, to a kind of sadness I still feel sometimes now. Why? Did I never feel part of? Why? Did I never feel good enough? Was there always this ailment malady, chase me up down an over. I don't fully know. What I do know now is about being powerless and being unable to manage my life. Then? It was as I have said whatever you could and did get away with was aces, romping stomping self will run riot. Yeah, cliches and slogans, but tell you what, going back in 50 year jumps, a lot now is what it is because of what I was, not what anyone did to me, or any of that o poor me bullshit. You pays your money and you takes your chances, sometimes ya win sometimes ya lose sometimes ya get a few years in a cell to contemplate the error of ya ways. A bit of one my sand mantras is no matter what I do it never seems good enough.

AND WE BOTH KNOW WHAT LOVE CAN BRING

Being half Irish saved me from ever being a so-called made man. However, I did get to sit down at the Italian American Social Club on 16th Street in Coney Island with some guys who knew me since I was a kid. Those years and those stories; stories about Neptune's Arms, Tommy the Whale, Louie Three Fingers, Mi Mi Patrilo, my cousin Ali Boy, and some others. One of the best tales was about this buddy of mine from Sea Gate who would go on to play pro football, and this deal with some kid whose father was indeed a made man, and the kid made some wisecracks about the football guy's sister, and I did not let him beat that kid up but took him to Neptune and had Tommy the Whale talk to him about it. The guy was built like a cinder block and Tommy the Whale knew his father, who worked for the mob. Tommy told his father, "You let me handle this, it'll be worse on that fucking goofball-eating shit-for-brains kid than any beat-down you could a throw him." Tommy the Whale handled it. And that was that.

Another time one of the guys asked me about Vietnam, and bless my cousin, who said, "He don't talk about that and I don't want him to talk about that." The guy never asked me about Vietnam again. And that was that.

I would later have a visit in San Francisco from Richie, and as the tale unfolds, Richie left me a big bag,of really good cocaine, on spec, and this would be the beginning of the way things fell apart.

But when I look at the good times up on Elsie Street, spending time with my new baby girl, and working on top-of-the-line cars, I know I need to write a few pages about that part of my life.

Around that time was when I got a job at Torelli Import Auto. I went to the Sears at Army Street and Mission and bought myself one of those little gray toolboxes with a basic selection of tools. Very basic. Then I drove over to Fell Street, and walked up the ramp with my toolbox, and Nick Torelli was standing there. "I need a job, I know a lot about cars but it's been a while since I've done that kind of work."

He is about 5'6" at most, but his words are sturdy. "Where have you been?" I told him how I just got back from Vietnam a little more than a year ago, and now I am living here. He asked me my name and made this funny face. "Your name is Albanese? My mom told me there was a feud between your family and mine in the old country." I told him I didn't know anything about that but since I spent about three years killing people I promised not to kill him if he gives me a job. And we both laugh. He said I could start the following Monday.

"I've got a guy moving on. Come meet Alfredo. He'll work with you until I see what you've got."

And that would lead to another lifelong friendship with a brother-teacher-mentor and all-around great guy. He was from a very rich family in Columbia. He was a civil engineer by training but could do anything he put his mind to. He was short and very round but had the most talented pair of hands I ever witnessed. I would work there from '68 to '71. It was good work, and those were good days. I still have that little gray toolbox.

Here is some more about that first real auto repair job at Torelli Import Auto and the year leading up to my daughter being born. Her mom and I lived in what to both of us was splendor up on Elsie Street. Back before the NYC days in '66 when I met her, she had been a Freedom Rider in Mississippi when I was off in Vietnam. Her father was Dr. Ben Keen, a well known and brilliant Latin American History professor who had been blackballed by McCarthy due to his friendship in Mexico with Trotsky and Rivera. I fell in love with his daughter, and I love her to this day. Splendor? Yes. On top of the hill with a front yard view from Noe Valley to downtown Frisco; on clear days we could see the bay and the bridge over to Oakland.

On Elsie Street lived some others who would factor into how we were able to raise our daughter. Neighbors being neighbors. The co-ops and swapping baby clothes and all of that. My income was decent. Plus the kickbacks on side deals. I was still selling lids of Panama Red and Mexican and Colombian weed. I still had access to kilos of it but now they cost me sixty percent more than what I paid in my cross-country days. Nick was pretty okay with all that long as the exchanges were not made in the shop.

Alfredo was not okay with it—not at all—so all of us kept that very hush-hush but never fooled him. "Your eyes are so red," he would say, and we would tell him there was too much chlorine in the pool at the YMCA that morning.

"You shit-for-brains. None of you fool me. Not for a second. Never let anything interfere with the work."

I had been working at the shop for over a month, and during that time all I did was chase parts, clean parts, put away tools, get tools, clean up and do whatever I was told to do. One morning I walked up the ramp and ran into Alfredo. He was not dressed for work. He looked me over and said, "Well, since you don't smell like you've been smoking that shit, go take out the motor in that Jaguar MK2 and I'll be back later." I thought I had died and gone to heaven.

I got Mike Tobin to help me take off the hood and then began the greater task. I had watched and helped Alfredo take out some other motors from MGs and some other cars. By mid-afternoon I had removed all the hoses and wires and bolts that needed to be removed. I had taken out the radiator connections and linkage, unbolted the transmission. As I was walking to get the cherry picker, Nick came out of the office, looked over, and came to help me. Not something he did very often for any of us. But he knew I was still a bit green, and a scratch or a dent or some other fuck-up would cost him money.

I set the chain in place. Nick tells me to put the floor jack under the transmission. As we lift the engine out, we clear the output shaft by moving the motor forward and tilting it up. The transmission settles on the jack. It comes out clean but leaks a bit of coolant that I blot with sawdust. We don't have a motor stand, so we place the motor on top of a fifty-five-gallon barrel. Alfredo shows back up and says, "Go home. I'll bring an extra motor stand in the morning, and you will take apart what I tell you to take apart and leave alone what I tell you to leave alone." How funny is that?

That car belonged to a doctor who had it overhauled before trading it for an XKE. That doctor would some months later deliver my daughter in exchange for me doing a clutch job for him. He paid for the parts. Life was very good, It takes time to get time, a long-held view of being in recovery. And time itself? I sit here all these years later, going back over, and stack it all up. All of it.

Memories of moments and long stretches. Of people and places and things. Between being in Frisco full-time from '68 to '86, to when I got sober and moved to Oregon, where I became of all things an Orthodox Church groundskeeper. Suddenly I was learning things that either I had ignored or were blocked from me by what is now called PTSD. I stack it all up. The late 60s through the mid-70s when we lived on Elsie Street. Me and my wife and our daughter.

Once, Carlos Santana and his percussionist Chepito drove up the ramp in a '58 Bentley that had smoke pouring from the hood and an odd noise coming from the engine. There was another Carlos who had a Porsche Speedster in there at the same time. I never really got to know Santana but I did know Chepito, and the other Carlos is a friend of mine to this day.

Alfredo took out the Bentley engine and sent it to Sammy Hale, one of the best machinists at the time. I helped Alfredo take out the engine, and when it came back, I helped Alfredo put it back in.

Then came the day when a young woman whose beauty could stop time walked into the shop. She walked up to me at the top of the ramp and said, "I'm in a big hurry, get the Bentley ready to be picked up." She then handed me fifty $100 bills. Back then $5000 was big money for one job. Big Roger had been watching and came over from his own space where he rebuilt VW engines. "Don't even tell me you know that woman," said Big Roger. I fanned the money at him and said, "She paid me for a hell of a good time last night." We both just cracked up. I went up to the office to give Scotty the money. Scotty was the shop's accountant and very attractive. When I hand her the money, she said "I know you want in my pants but it's gonna take more than that."

The end of my time at Elsie Street was near. My wife wanted to go to New Mexico for what I was told was more work on her second PhD, but in truth she was running off with another man and wanted me to take care of our daughter for what she said would be less than a year. It turned out to be more than three years. I had to move to North Beach and get an apartment across the alley from my best pal Ed, so he could watch Mary after school while I was still working. By that time, I was already at Ferrari of SF, a job Alfredo got me. The shop on Fell Street was closing up and Nick replaced it with a junkyard. Alfredo partnered with his brother Juan at Continental Motors, a shop that exists to this day.

Sooner than later, the taxman and city government locked up Ferrari of SF for reasons having to do with money. I had the keys to the side door and entered the shop to get my tools out of there. I went to work for Giles Yee at Grant Avenue

Garage half a block from where Mary and I lived. At the top of Filbert Street is Garfield Elementary School where Mary was a student from second through fourth grade. Some of the most pleasant memories of all those years are the ones in which she comes down the hill from school and stops by the garage to visit me at work.

Ed converted a closet in his apartment into a little room for Mary, with a TV and couch and small desk. Mary loved it there. Ed's daughter Ana and her friend Leslie helped me so much. They were about six or so years older than Mary and treated her like a little sister. Sometimes Mary would window-shop the stores on Grant Avenue. Giles saw her a few times in front of a store that had a pair of green sparkle sneakers in the window display. One day she drops by the shop to visit me, and Giles calls her over and hands her a shoebox containing the sneakers.

She wore those shoes out. The two women who did the paperwork at the shop were nice to Mary as well. They took her out to eat a few times and bought her toys and her first Hello Kitty accessories. Then her mother returned. Two of my friends helped me gather Mary's possessions.

As memory changes time to time, in a jump back.

Due in part to how my brain works, when I am in one place in time here and another time place person is all of a sudden the video in my mind. It came to me, about a confession or a memory jog. I have been all the things I said I was, and without saying who what and where even when it does move from place year or like that, I know what really counted and what needs to be either forgot or just left on the note book page. Between time and place.

Sheila Kane back in NYC is good a spot to start as anyplace. I had written her letters and poems from Vietnam; she was a high school friend of my friend, John (Maddy) Madison. She wrote me back, and I was told that she lived with two other women at 257 E 72nd on the corner of 2nd Ave. I even remember the phone number: 212 249 1229. She would go to Gleason's pub on 1st Ave and read some of the poems I wrote. I do not have any of those letters or poems now. I called her from a pay phone in the Port Authority terminal and asked her if I could come stay at her place till I got my own apartment. She said yes, and I walked with a duffle bag to her place. I do not feel like saying the other two women's names, but I have spoken to one of them last year or so. Sheila died a few years ago. The window, looking out on 2nd Ave became my bower, my safe spot, and as I recall I stayed there for almost a month. I would stand on the corner, at the red light, and wait for a truck with a back ledge, sit on it, and go down to the Lower East Side. I had no purpose, no real motivation, other than to somehow adjust to civilian life, and the fact of what would turn into about 15 or so years of madness.

I know I did not meet Patricia first. A guy I knew from Coney Island did. He told me he saw her in line somewhere in Manhattan; there was something about her eyes he told me, that he just knew she was someone I would fall in love with. This is going to sound all hippie dippy, but I was in Tomkins Square Park, she was sitting on a bench, and I knew it was her, soon as I walked by. I have never really tried to figure that part out, but I knew it was her.

"Excuse me, did you meet a guy named George yesterday in the store line, and he told you about me?" She was, I am pretty sure, not ready to even talk to me. I was not dirty or smelly, but it was obvious she was guarded. I reached out my hand and introduced myself as the guy he mentioned to her and fresh out of the Army and at a loss of how George knew I was supposed to meet you. I then sat down, and she told her name and that she was herself recently moved to NYC. She had spent a couple of years in Mississippi as a freedom rider and civil rights activist. I was impressed and told her so. Unsure of what was to happen, I asked her if I could take her out to dinner and we might get to know each other better. She said yes, but had to do some work that afternoon, could we meet here at about 6PM. I said I will be here, and I hope you come. I went back uptown and told Sheila, "I think I met someone today and if it turns out the way I think it is going to, I will be moving soon."

She did not ask me much, but without saying my welcome was getting thin, and I knew it was time to move on anyway. So, out comes my best pair of pants, a clean shirt, and off I go. Patricia was on the bench when I got there, and I was not nervous, but determined to act right and win her heart. We went to Manero's steak house, a rather fancy and high-class place. Good conversations.

If only I'd known how far down the shit-chute I would fall. Driving the souped-up VW bus, running dope across the country. That would end with me trading the motor out of the last van for a bag of Bolivian marching powder, parking the body of the van outside Nick's junkyard and living in it for about three months, then taking a job offered to me in Oregon at a Ferrari dealer. Living in a van, taking showers at the Y, eating very little, practically about to kill myself, wide-eyed and aimless, walking through the city at night.

Knocking over small scores of all sorts of things. All on a bicycle. And so on and so forth. One time, I knocked over the bicycle, then stood looking at it and considering it. Then I lifted it from the ground. In the city at night a person can be almost invisible moving through the streets on a bicycle. Nobody pays attention. Not even the cops. I rode the bicycle all night. It would be stolen out of my van. I miss it to this day. Again, moving around place and time is how I think and remember and how I write. In and out of those years, not all that concerned about consecutive order.

I am working at Ferrari of SF, and this guy pulls up in a red 308. He gets out and is wearing a fancy coat. Johannes is standing next to me and says, "That's a Russian sable coat. It costs as much as the car does."

I look over and say, "Yeah, this guy is a poster boy for the rich and flashy."

The poster boy says the car needs a tune-up and some other tuning up. "Just fix whatever needs to be fixed," he says. He leaves and is picked up at the curb by a woman who looks like a fashion model driving a new Cadillac.

I take the car out for a run up and down Van Ness Avenue, just feeling it and listening to it. It has a bit of loose steering or a low tire. I'm not sure which. I take it back to the shop and the shop assistant helps me take off the cowl cover for the engine. I drain out all the fluids and take off the air cleaner and the velocity stacks. The next day, I take off the valve covers and run a feeler gauge to check all the clearances. Six valves are a bit tight, and I make a reading of the shims with a micrometer. I button up the valve covers, take off the cover of the transaxle bearings and check each of them for any sign of heat or a loose clearance. I then replace all the fluids, bleed the whole brake system. I check the brakes, the wheels and tires, and all the bearings closely. One tire is chopped and a bit slack. No need to ask, just replace the two front tires and use a bubble level to check the alignment. No loose steering parts. All the shocks and bushings are okay except for one on the passenger front and that must be how the tire got chopped. Replace it. Leave the back hood engine cover off and take it out for a rather spirited road test. Up Bay Street into the Marina District and then almost to the Golden Gate Bridge. I turn off and come back the Marina way. Three pretty girls look at the car, and with the air cleaner still off it sounds like a race car. The girls wave and blow kisses, and I wave and keep moving. I'm coming up on Green St and nail the brakes to make sure there's no fade or any movement out of the suspension. Something hits my foot. It's a 9mm pistol, in what looks like a very expensive clip-on holster.

 I get back inside the shop and look under both seats. Under the driver's seat is the pistol and a bag of cocaine. Under the passenger seat is a deposit envelope with what feels like a big wad of cash. I am sorely tempted to take the dope and the money, but I don't. I refit the air cleaner assembly and the engine cover. Jose gives the car a nice wash and wax job and parks it in the same line the new cars are in.

 No one arrives on Friday to pick up the car. Saturday comes and goes. I watch the Sunday evening news and a breaking story about a major art forgery case. And there he is. Mr. Russian Sable coat in handcuffs coming down the steps of some Atherton mansion.

 I am beside myself. I had the keys to the shop side door, and head to the shop. I take the gun and the dope and the money and put all of it in my toolbox. Well, not all of it. I helped myself to a few spoonfuls of the coke before loading the bag into my toolbox.

Monday. The FBI shows up looking for the car. I take Dino into the parts room and show him the dope and the money, we hoot up a few lines and it's very good dope. Plus $3700 in cash, and the pistol I can sell it for about a grand. As it worked out I had not spent any of the money or sold the gun.

All of this, the dealership going down in tax cheating flames, Dino and Johannes opening their own shop, and Dino only living a short time after it all. All of it in and out of focus, as I move through memory, from hole to hole. I called Dino's lady partner and offered her some money. She thanked me and said it was all good. Turns out Dino was way more rich then I knew and he did talk about me and our time in Italy; she said he really did love me. He was only in his 30s. He complained about a pain in his neck and back, went into the hospital on a Monday and died on that Wednesday.

The house on the hill, the wife, the daughter. Patty and I had lived there now for just about more than one year. When we moved in, Rick and Ida had left this eight-foot high, five-foot wide wooden box that was a desk, with a set of shelves and a JBL speaker fitted in the bottom. On the front was a drawing of Edgar Allan Poe, drawn by Steve Raines, who I had met on my first tour of that house some years ago. Rick had also left some LP records. I went down to Market Street and bought a Nikko stereo with a turntable, and a buddy of mine set it up to use the JBL speaker as well.

Oh, the music of those days. Quicksilver Messenger Service, Jefferson Airplane, Janis Joplin, Gary McFarland (eighty miles an hour through beer can country), Miles

Davis, Mingus and Gillespie. In the kitchen, an old wooden ice box and a butcher's block for a counter. There was also a backroom with a dirt floor, where Rick had left a giant pile of posters on a long table. That table would later be used by Crumb, Wilson, Spain, and Moscoso to create the All-Star Jam drawings for Zap Comix. 1969-1974 or so.

Rick had left Texas and was now living in San Clemente but would come up and stay with us. The Zap boys would come over and smoke up a bunch of weed and draw their asses off. In November of '69 my daughter was born. Joey and Jennifer Komlos lived upstairs, and Jennifer was the one who took Patty to the hospital, called me at work, and I tore over there. Funny enough, it was the French Hospital on Geary Boulevard, and some twenty-three years before I had been born in the French Hospital on 10th Avenue in NYC. I had traded with Dr. Moss and in exchange for a job on his car he delivered my baby. I get to the hospital and the nurse puts me in medical coveralls with a mask. I go in the delivery room and see Patty up on the table and that's when I fainted dead away. Jennifer just cracks up and says, "Big ass war hero," and I low-crawled out the swinging door.

When the nurse brought Mary and Patty out on the rolling bed, it was a moment in my life I will never forget. That little wrinkled-up, good-sized baby girl. It should've been enough to change me. More than enough. And for about two years it did. I was a good baby daddy, and we had all sorts of assistance from the other Bernal Heights hippie families who had babies too. Joel and Carolyn, and some others. Joey and Jennifer had two kids but a bit older. I was all about working and I kept any of my weed dealing very low key, and again for about the first two years of Mary's life, it was idyllic and so sweet. Patty used to bake cakes and sell them to the Cooking Company in North Beach, and I used to take Mary over there in the van. They all fell in love with her. She was (and is to this day) one of the most reasonable people I have ever known. There was a time there, a bit later, when I would take her for rides on my motorcycle. One day when she was about four years old, she comes out and says, "Nope." She never wanted to ride on that motorcycle again. I am lost here, I really am, in the mix and chronology of what happened and when. It all comes together and comes apart.

I was working at Torelli Import, and the whole crew there bought a bunch of baby toys. When Patty was really well along, she said walking was really good for her. We would walk down Virginia Avenue to the Safeway on Mission and going back uphill I used to push her to help her along.

What a sweet memory that is. That home, 101 Elsie Street, was a bit of life at its best. Nothing can change those early years.

In passing, here and now, I can shadow the parts I choose to include. Oh, dear. There was a woman who was on Elsie Street for a time. She was a Russian translator for the UN. We had what we had, some of it with regrets, but in time she and I became close friends. Oh, man. All those years ago. I can see the places and hear the sounds. That old shovel-head chopper, and down the next block lived Sweet William, who Lenore Kandel wrote *The Love Book* about. I helped him build a blue pan-head chopper, and he and I had some dope days, and last time I saw him we were both in prison.

A book, a tome, a memoir that includes the clouds and fog of memory. Have any of us lived times that were both profound and crazy? I bet some of us, probably all of us, and sadly only a few of us ride through it and write it down.

Sweet William was a righteous bad ass. He was a Hell's Angel, a poet, a thinker, and doer. It was a dope house in Oakland in the 70's, a tale of crime and how some bikers would sell a kilo of cocaine to some black guys, then go back and steal their money, even though they had already paid for the dope. It was out somewhere near Seminary Park. I was parked on a side street as a back-up. Four guys went in, and William took three 9mm shots to his body. Two guys carried him out and laid him across the bike and took him to a doctor who took the money and kept his mouth shut.

Sweet William was never the same. He couldn't ride the pan-head chopper anymore, so we stripped the bike and sold off the parts and built him a VW-powered trike. He would come to my house on Precita Street, with really good cocaine that he would buy from another guy named Dominic who lived up on Potrero Hill. He brought me a copy of his Hell's Angels book, *Memento Mori*, and it included a poem about me. We got pie-eyed loaded, parked his trike in my garage, and I took him home to Winfield Street, then picked him up the next day to ride off to what would turn out to be a time both of us would get locked up, the last time I would ever see him.

One would do well to remember that in Frisco in those days of the late 60's through the 70's were poets and artists and musicians who were all about letting it all hang out, if it feels good do it, until, sadly–as Hunter S. Thompson and George Carlin would later say–it all became the same old capitalist game; all of it became all about money. And I made some pretty good money selling posters and handbills from

The Family Dog and Bill Graham concerts, and I went to any concert free of charge.

Around the same time, my life was coming apart at the seams. Dope, money, guns. I started doing late night break-ins. Gas stations, restaurants, bars. Break open the safe, steal the money, buy cocaine. I have a memory block from those times. I want to call it the result of misadventure and anger and acting out PTSD, but in truth it was the result of a sad and deep addiction. My vocabulary shrank to one word: More.

My wife left me and moved with our daughter to 20th Street in the Mission. She rented a nice apartment, and in the building were some women who were the vanguard of feminism. They bought my daughter Big Wheel. I have a sweet memory of calling Mary while Al and I were at La Rondalla on the corner of Valencia Street and 20th having dinner.

Mary rode her Big Wheel over and sat with us. Carlos, the owner of the restaurant, made a small plate of nacho chips for Mary. All of this while I was working at Ferrari and in and out of dazed drug states. Even now, all these years later, it's hard to make it all about what was good, because in truth all of it was crashing down.

Going to prison saved my life. I had only seen freebasing and crack; I had never tried them. If I would've tried them, I would've died. That's a fact. I saw seven guys who went from bodybuilders to skeletons and died with a spike in their arm or a glass pipe on the floor where someone found them.

In an aside, had someone told me 38 years ago when my life was a walking toilet bowl, my big worry would be my swimming pool over the top or my enclosure screens blow off...yeah, easy to see the parallels between living in an old hulk of a VW van to where I live now. As much as I am more than willing to do both what I think needs doing and doing it the best I can, I don't have a big concern about time, only about quality and I think keep it short tight and with both image and events of *Then N Now*...................unto the ages of ages

No beginning, no middle, no end.

Going back over some old notebooks, and some rather dreadful poetry, then finding this other notebook with twenty-seven pages written in pencil by Linda on a Greyhound bus from Frisco to NYC, and titled, "Leaving SF with Tearful Eyes." Linda lived upstairs on Elsie Street for a year or two. She was involved with my best pal Spain, and he and I always said we'd never mess with each other's girlfriends, but I knew her before he did, and in fact I introduced them to each other. I loved her from the second I met her. I was alone then, downstairs. Patty and Mary had moved out. Linda and I used to sit on the stairs and look at the fog roll in over Twin Peaks and make up stories about the people in the houses in Noe Valley that we could no longer see.

We laughed and rolled in it. We had a set of secret identities: Herman and Helga McBernanici. Linda was a writer for the SF Mime Troupe, and the whole collection of them would come over and have picnics in the yard. Andrea Snow, the woman who played the Dragon Lady, is to this day a very dear pal of mine. How funny she married Larry Adelman.

And going back, when Spain and Linda broke up, Linda and I carried on for months. We used to go to bed and call it Beat the Clock. We broke two beds on Coso Street where she had gotten the top floor apartment. Then she met Gene and married him, but when she came back alone we carried on again.

When she went back and they were driving somewhere, she would point out old cars. Later she would tell me he said, "You've been fucking that ginny bastard car mechanic again, ain't ya?" He and I never met, and later on, during a phone call, she said, "I'm not comfortable talking now." She got a brain tumor and died. Andrea and Larry called me, but I already somehow knew. I really did. One of the saddest things I ever wrote was:

> *After weeks of mourning I can say good*
> *bye, sail on silver bird sail on high*
> *I love you Linda I always have*
> *and will till the day I die.*

Between her, and my moving out to North Beach with my daughter for three years, there were a few others. Then I met the woman who would be the love of my life, and as sad as it is, I fucked that up too. In the early parts of my total downfall, she left never to return with "I love you too much to see you destroy yourself." And so it goes. Life and time.

In another episode, I took a woman skydiving, and had to tandem jump her, and we both laughed later that night at her saying, "Hey big boy I'm on top now. Move that ass of yours so I can free fall again."

One day, any day, in a series of days, now so long ago. An Army buddy of mine called Torelli Imports and asked for me. He and I chatted a bit about who was still alive, where they were, and then he said to me, "There's a woman mechanic here who wants to move to the Bay Area. Can you hook her up with a job?" I told him I would try, and said, "Tell her to look me up."

About three weeks later, Marsha shows up early one morning at the shop. She asks Mike, who greeted her, "Who is Dominic?" To this day, I can remember him saying, "I don't know. It depends on the day or the mood he's in, but that's him over there."

She comes over, tells me she's a friend of Sal, that they had worked together in Boston. She looks like a schoolteacher and has what looks to me like delicate hands. I told her I knew she was looking for work. I asked her if she was a good mechanic and what her pay scale was. She said, "I can do anything any man can do and I usually do it cleaner and faster. I get $19 an hour now." I go up to the office and talk with Nick. First off, he's not really interested, and says, "Yeah, women in the shop. It's all I can do to keep all you horn dogs away from Scotty and Laurel." I tell Nick that Sal would never send me a ringer.

I tell him to at least give her a shot. "I have an MGB that I'm about to do a clutch job on. Let her either help me or do it herself, then you make up your mind."

We go back down. She is standing in my stall. I ask her, "Have you ever put a new clutch in an MG?" She laughs and says, "A few." I ask her if she has work clothes and would she be willing to do this one. She goes back down the ramp, comes back with a pair of coveralls and work shoes, goes into the bathroom and changes. I was at that time also building two motorcycles. One for Nick and one for Ernie the painter. She pulls out the jack and four stands, and I watch how she jacks it up and places the stands, and I tell her she can use my tools. On the bench she had already laid out just about everything it takes to do that job. I am busy doing the wires and setting up the frame engine and transmission, and not paying much attention to her. I hear the MGB start up, and look over, and she has the hose on the tailpipe, and it is blowing out the rubber squares we had in the walls. Again, I do not know how much time passed but it is not yet time for lunch. If she is done, she has beat the time it takes me to do one.

She turns off the engine and lowers down the car. Nick comes down and gets in the car, looks at the shift lever and feels the free play in the pedal.

He gets out and takes the drop-light and looks over the bell housing and since the car is already down on the floor, he gets in and drives it down the ramp.

She puts my tools away, and Nick drives back up, tells me to go park it in the lot, and he and Marsha go upstairs. I walk back in and she gives me a hug. Nick hired her. She says that shipping her tools out would take about a week, and that Nick said he would pay for shipping. I told her she could use my tools until hers arrived.

I kind of got to add here there was an unspoken tension in the shop about who is going to hit on her and how. Other than Al, we are all pretty crass. I told her about the bikers and the other assortments of people who had their cars worked on here, and that it was no cafe society crowd.

Again how memory is clear and not, but I can hear her say, "Dom, I am a gay woman, and I also can fight and shoot if I have to, and if you think this crowd is hard ass you should have been in Boston on the south end and met some them assholes." We bonded at that moment. I would only work with her for about four months, because this was about the same time Alfredo got me the job at Ferrari. Of course, I would still come by the shop and see my pals and talk to Nick and Marsha. Nick told me, in his sarcastic way, "She out-works you. She has zero come backs. And I hear you're Mr. Fancy Pants now with those high-dollar cars." I felt dumped, but I also knew Nick was going to close shop within the year. He had bought into two junkyards out in Hunters Point.

Marsha and I went to lunch, and I told her that evening I would take her and introduce her to Kathleen who with her brother had a repair and body shop on 17th Street in the Mission. I said to her that I bet they would get along famously.

Well, all that happens, and as it turned out, Kathleen was in love with Sammy Hale the machinist, and she and one of her other woman friends were going to open up their own shop on Folsom Street, and from there Marsha Derrida and Kathleen became not only famous but got really rich as well. They did amazing work and were part of a deal called The Arcane Car Club. All kinds of odd three-wheelers, micro-cars, anything that was odd and rare, they either had one or worked on one. It was something to see.

I could go on, and I think I will.

Those days at Torelli Import Auto are a bit in and out of my memory. When Nick died, I was in San Fran for six months to help his widow settle the estate. I had met her when they got married, about four years before, and told some of the Torelli Import stories at the wedding dinner and people cracked up. Here's a great one.

Nick knew these two German guys in Marin who had a body shop, Klaus and Horst. They had two cousins from Hungary who they had smuggled into the USA on some bogus paper. Both of them were ace mechanics, even if neither of them was four-and-a-half-feet tall. Nick would call the body shop and tell Klaus and Horst what he wanted done, they would translate, and the two cousins would show up at the shop in the evening and do whatever. We would have a motor out of a Triumph TR3, and we would come into the shop in the morning, and Nick had laid out the parts or the new head or whatever, and the motor would be all ready to go back in the car. Nick told us, "My elves." We just laughed and shook our heads and figured Nick was coming in at night and doing the work himself.

Around 3AM one morning, Mike Tobin and I are coming home from a jazz club. We had been drinking booze and smoking hash, and both of us were half drunk and half stoned. We turn up Fell Street and see two little people leaving the shop. Mike almost crashes the Austin Cambridge into a parked car. We both sit there and see the two little guys get into a VW Bug and drive away. When I told that story at the wedding, some of the guests nearly spat out their drinks.

It was a lot of fun at that garage. Women? Yes. Dope? Yes. But no hard stuff. There was a guy who shipped in big dinner plates of Afghan hash in a Land Rover. They hanged him in Iran. His buddy Massod told us, "Hassan is gone. I need the money from that last load to pay his family."

Nick, bless him, and he did not want to give up the hash, went up to the safe and paid it off. We smoked so much of that stuff you could hear us coughing in the bathroom. Al did not like it, but would not bust our chops about it, as long as the work got done.

Then, in '72 I go to Ferrari of SF, and there are some tales out of there. I am doing some due diligence on my facts versus my memory. In fact, I just got off the phone with Johannes in San Mateo where he has a Ferrari shop, and he told me it was as I remembered it, that the Ferrari of SF got closed down for tax fraud and our mutual buddy the service manager was beating his feet to Costa Rica with the FBI, DEA, IRS, and the California cops on his ass. He never came back.

I have read and learned through being in recovery for so long, that fear of abandonment and self-esteem issues are the similarities we look for, not the difference, and how we all came to give up only to move on. One of those days, early after my daughter was born in 1969, I would hold her, and feed her with the bottle, and burp her on my shoulder and wonder how many other fathers with a new baby girl have just sat and held her, and loved her, and felt some agony about bringing her into this world. All these many years later, when she is now going on fifty-three, and is a part of my life so long now, even if there were some estranged years. I can remember when Patty told me she and Mary were moving out, she had had enough of me, and my life started coming apart at the seams due to my own letting it all become about a life of petty crime and guns and motorcycles.

That fucking war in Vietnam, that I had not even processed or faced up to my own guilt and shame. No matter that back in NYC before Patty and I came to Frisco, I was very involved in the Vietnam Vets against the war. In fact, I am a founding member of that. No real rancor or any of that "if I had to do it over again" stuff. Though I would've been way better about child support and maybe had a better set of standards and morals to guide me.

The hardest thing is writing about who and how you used to be, compared to who and how you are now. That whole idea about the folly of youth. One day drunk and stoned, I downshifted my chopper at 80mph, blew the gear box up, gear oil on the rear tire, and fell over, sliding sideways down the freeway for 100 or more yards. Traffic going by, not one mark on me, and I lift up the bike, kickstand it on the shoulder, walk home about three miles away, get my old 50 Dodge pickup with a ramp and a small winch, put the bike in the bed, go home and pass out. The next day I get up and take the bike to Frisco Chopper and me and Spider put in a new gear box. We do some other work on it, and it cost me about $300. For a week, I drove the truck to work and back, then I had to go get the bike.

My roommate Jan drives the truck back home. She is just loving that truck. I get home from work, and she is sitting at the kitchen table and says, "If you don't wanna ride your bike take my VW, because as of today that truck is mine." Later she would move over to Berkeley without the truck.

Since Nick had pretty much given me that truck, I gave it to a kid who Nick liked, a kid who Nick helped open his own painting business, and to the best of my knowledge that kid kept that truck for over thirty or more years. Who and how you used to be. Balance and factor in the good, the bad, the ugly. All of it. I heard one time that no one ever does to you something you did not do already to someone else.

Balance? I bet a few good moves I made got me out of a few jams.

The history of that particular chopper is particular to my history. Back then I never had anything registered or legal, that bike was in Nick's name, so after a few other close calls I told him it was time to sell it and he agreed. We went to the local Harley dealer, and they offered $2,500 for it. Nick and I talked it over. We didn't have $500 invested in it. It was built from either stolen or otherwise accumulated parts. He says to me, "You'd just piss away the money, so here I'm gonna give you this Fiat 1100D. It's up to date and registered to the junkyard." I drove that car for a lot of years, then asked Nick to transfer it to a buddy of mine moving east. The buddy not only drove it to Boston, he overhauled it and drove it till he died in 2000.

Looking back, it was a good ride. All of it. I want these pages to have clarity and sense, as I write about a time when I didn't have much of either.

A 1964 conversation, in a mortar pit on the wire line in a camp, Gia Vuc, Vietnam. Smoke a bit of Cambodian Red and drink some almost cold San Miguel beer. Best I can recall. Maddy and I are talking it out. "Mad Dog, what is the worst could happen?"

"Monk San, we get killed."

No quick comeback for that.

"So, what is the best could happen?"

With half a bottle gone in a swig and a burp, he says, "We live, we go back to the land of the Big PX with them big tit round-eyed women and get really cool motorcycles."

I got the drift of it all posthaste.

I told him about my family, about my home life. And he told me about his. His were the opposite of mine. His dad was a lawyer. He had sisters and a brother, and they all went to good schools. He was handsome. A bit of a wise guy. He was well endowed. Always saying he had to go "drain the monster." Plus a few side jokes aimed at me, and that was okay.

I told him about Elsie Street, and in a rather long and drawn out back and forth, I remember him saying to me,

"I think that's a fantasy you cooked up, you're going back to a rat ass bungalow on some backstreet in Coney Island."

I didn't get defensive. In my own mind back then, all of Frisco was sort of a pipe dream. I knew if I did go home, I would have to see my dad and my brothers, and be in NYC, because that was where I knew people and where I knew how to make money. Or for sure knew people who did. How it seems to wander just like my brain does in try to collect and record the days, times and people and places.

All those cool talks we used to have, half lit, interspersed with combat alley patrols and guys getting killed. And me with my own mental footlocker full of dreams. I was going to live through this. I was going to live in that two-story green wooden house, no matter what.

I think one of the best lines I ever wrote was:
> *You cannot aid the dead, the holes they*
> *leave in the living is the hard part.*

When things were good on Elsie Street, they were pretty damn good. A friend of mine just posted a photo of that house in its present condition. It's painted brown with all new windows and doors, and all I hear is it sold for $1.3 million nearly fifteen years ago. What was a big yard on either side of it is now replaced with houses.

Anyhow. I was working at Torelli Imports, and Nick had become the slang term, "a piece of work." He knew about money and had his fingers in a lot of pies. Stolen Porsches that he would convert to E production race cars called Flower Power. That and some side dope deals. I mentioned Hassan, who smuggled in the dinner plate pounds of the best Afghan hash. He did it in a Land Rover that had bolted-down floors, between the real frame and the floor he had added another one that would hold about twenty of the dinner plates. Nick used to get one on the house for off-loading them and passing them back, and in the meantime selling us some of his and keeping some for himself. It went on for I think more than a year, then came cocaine. Nick was not a big user, but saw how he could get it free, because he had a safe full of money.

Tony Sparkle used to come over from North Beach with like six ounces that went for about $3,000 a pop. Nick would buy all six for $2,750, send me to the bike shop with five of them, on the front for $2,900 each, and once they were stepped on five of them became seven, and a big profit.

It took less than a week, and I would pick up the money and I never took a dime, but Nick would dip into his and give me a few spoonfuls. It was fun till it was no fun no more at all.

Alfredo's brother, Juan, opened a car shop on California Street. There was a Chinese woman named Mi Lee, who had a 140 Jaguar fix-head coupe. She was very wealthy and loved driving and cars. She looked over at the squat black Mini Cooper that Al had built for himself, a hot rod, Mill tune engine and disk brakes and it was, even with the small wheels and tires, a go go mobile. She said she wanted one like that. Al knew of one that was pretty cherry and not used now at all. He made the deal for it, it was a light blue and bare bones stock. She did not want that; she wanted it gloss black like his, and re-done like his. Money was not an issue at all, so Al told her it would take about 3 months and she told him to sell the Jag and keep the money; if it was more, she would pay that too. A guy came and picked her up, she left the jag and the title.

Al had me take all the running gear out of the Mini Cooper, and leave the wheels on it and have it towed to the body shop for a full down to bare metal and re-paint. When it got to the body shop, I helped them put it on a flat wheel dolly and took off the wheels, brakes, and what was left of the front suspension. Back on California Street, in the back corner, were all the parts. Al had me take the motor apart and in a pickup bed take it to the machine shop. He came with me and told them just what he wanted. They had done his engine too. Better cylinder bore with dish pistons and the head re-machined for better valves and a dual intake manifold for the single draft carbs, and a polished crankshaft with way better main and rod bearings. When the body came back about month later, Al himself did the install of the better suspension parts and 4-wheel disk brakes with all new both metal and flex brake lines with a master cylinder that had dual feed with a proportional valve. The engine would not be back for weeks, so he took the combo transmission and differential all apart, and added better shafts gears and synchro. The axles were stouter; I do not remember how or where he got those. In the meantime, we were doing some other cars, and I did really enjoy coming over to help, and when I would show up in a Ferrari Al would, just like Nick used to tease me, call me Mr. Fancy Pants.

It all came together, and he had Caio from the body shop upstairs come and wax, polish, and make the paint and whole car look like brand new. I took a few days off from my job, it was towards the time that Ferrari dealer would go under anyhow. Al and I took the car out 3 times; he would really nail it and then come back and adjust this or that. It was in one day he took all the linkage apart and made it shift way crisp and not have any gear noise.

She came to the shop only one time during the overhaul while it was a bare body and was very pleased at the paint and the overall look. She never said a word about how much the Jag went for or how much this was all going to come to. Almost to the day, 3 months later it was ready for her. She came, and I almost choked when Al told me to take her for a ride. I did, but not dare drive it like Al had but I did on Bay St open it up from say 30 to 70 and it just flew. I pulled over and asked her if she wanted to drive back. She said no, she would drive it after she and Al did. All this comes back, and I cannot find today the jade necklace she gave me but I remember it well. In the next few days, she would go on like 5 rides with Al, and on 4 of them she did drive it back. Like a little kid she would giggle and just dance at how much she liked it. She took a driving class at Sears Point from Bob Bondurant before she came to take it home. The money talk or any of that I was not privy to. The last thing that happened was this guy showed up with a brand-new Lincoln Continental in dark green with a guy following him and tells Al, "Mi Lee wants to thank you deeply," and they gave Al the title and it was already in his name. The times and place all sort of meld now.

Upstairs was a body shop run by another Colombian named Caio, and a part-time body man there named Jack S., who would later become top dog of the SF narcotics squad and retire as Assistant Chief of Police. Back then he was a patrol man with a partner named Ernie Green, who had eyes to get on the narc squad because that is where a lot of side money can be made. Anyway, Jack tells Al's brother Juan that Ernie knows what is going on at Torelli, and Caio tells

Al, who tells Nick, and the fingers in the pies stop dead in their tracks.

Within a year of me getting a job at the Ferrari dealership, Nick would close shop and go on to have two junkyards. The move was an epic gangster move, about five cut-up race cars and, I'm going to say, around ten other cars that Nick found up in Noe Valley, owned by people who didn't use their garages, and he would lease and store them, his Aston Martin DB7 and a few Jaguar cars, and some odd-ass ones, like this Fiat Italia that was then not worth spit but would be years later, and a three-wheeled Reliant Robin that I got to drive around a bit. Way cool, and then he found this garage on Castro Street with room for a lot of cars and an area for a shop.

I was crazy then about this girl named Laurel Ann, not the same Laurel I had been involved with earlier, and she had a sister named Nancy whose Volvo needed a clutch job. I used Nick's tow-truck and took it to Castro Street. They both came over and watched me do the job. Nick came by, saw them, and later would say to me, "If you're dipping in either one of those, you're a better man than I ever thought you were." No, I never did, and Laurel went off with some wildlife photographer guy, up to Truckee. Oh, well. I lost touch with both of them.

A lot of years later, after Nick died, I found all his stashed cars and motorcycles. He had paid up the lease for years in the front. Some guy from England came and paid me almost 450K for a few cars and about twelve British bikes, one of which being a prototype Norton, and I never found out how Nick got his hands on that one. The others were all re-numbered stolen bikes that either me or one of my cohorts had stolen from rich kids up in the East Bay.

    Remember I told you about the stolen Porsches? One of Nick's last breath words to me was "Get Kruger," a guy who rented a shop from him and was a full-time pain in the ass about everything. Nick also owned a bathhouse on Silver Avenue with one of his junkyard partners. The last race car was in that bathhouse. So, I get an offer from a vintage race club up in Auburn, for 30 or 40K. I told them no and the Widow Torelli was furious. I told her to shut up, that I had this one. I went to see Kruger.

    I told him he could have Flower Power for 15K in cash, and in those days you got around the register by being off-road only, with no VIN or anything like that. So he says, "I want it.

    Where is it?" I tell him to pay me, and I will deliver it. Beside all of that, Nick's son Neil worked at Kruger's shop. I borrowed Big Roger's tow truck and delivered the car to Paul Street. Kruger paid Neil about a month's worth of wages just to get that car running again. It was not easy because the motor was fully tricked out, and the hydraulic system was kaput. It took almost three months to do it.

    The Revenge? Dumb ass Kruger takes it to the highway patrol to get one of those blue stickers so he could then go to the DMV and get paperwork for it. In running shape and all spiffed up the car is now worth anywhere from 50 to 75k. At the highway patrol station was a cop whose life's mission was finding old cold case stolen cars. I am back in Oregon by then, and the Widow Torelli calls me. "Where did that car come from?"

I told her I stole it in '68 or '69 in El Cerrito. The kicker was the doctor got his car back and Kruger got nothing. He tried to and the lawyer next door shut his ass down. With the bill of sale I cooked up, "sold as is, sold as scrap," there wasn't anything Kruger could do, especially since he had signed it. So I granted Nick his dying wish. I got Kruger.

More feedback on scatter shots and the ins and outs of both time and place. Well, I can only do this as the events trigger other ones, and in my own mind it is catch as catch can.

I was asked, "Do you not have a soul?"

The best I could reply was that I left it on a hill in Vietnam. No matter how much I have read about PTSD or other vets with similar problems, I never thought about any of that. My only conception of right or wrong was just not getting caught. Probably the most honest men I ever knew were my dad and Alfredo Caicedo, who was really my mentor and taught me how to do things. The next forty or more years would make me good pay and earn me some status as a top-of-the-line mechanic.

I go back now to Oakland, where Al and his brother Juan had this giant shop and yard. When I say giant, I mean half a block wide and long.

There was a scrap dealer named Mr. Brown, who would give Al the most amazing deals on surplus military stuff. Lathes, welders, even a D-8 Caterpillar bulldozer. He also gave him this big steel set of shelving, that was twenty feet high and forty feet wide. Me and a deaf guy named Claudio assembled them with a 4x4 wood A-frame, with a block and tackle chain and hook. When Mr. Brown came one day with a broken-down forklift, he was stunned. "How did you get that up there?" Al just laughed and said, "My donkeys they do what I say, I feed em, I even pay em sometimes, and if they don't obey me, I hit em so hard they need a cherry picker to get back up." A couple of years there back and forth across the Bay Bridge, sometimes in some swanky ass Ferrari or another car some collector let me play with.

Al would fix anything, build what he could not find, and that bulldozer? He and Claudio and I took it apart to the last bolt, then put it in a container and Al shipped it back to Colombia, where he would return to after a few years.

In the meantime, we took in a GMC pickup that had a loose sleeve in its #3 cylinder. The spark plug would blow out and it sounded like a machine gun. BAP BAP BAP. We pulled the head and rebuilt it. We used that pickup to tow the big Navy welder to a shop in Frisco where Al was going to weld up a frame. I'm on the welder riding it like an iron horse with the taillights and brake lights strapped. We welded up the frame, and the guy at the shop took pity on us and lent us his wrecker with a winch. Al took the pickup and I drove the wrecker back, with the welder attached. Then walked a few miles to where I had a Fiat in someone's garage. All of this comes to me both in and out of time. Scattershot feedback. I cannot really keep track of the days and months and years.

We worked on a lot of interesting cars. Al got this Horch, a prewar, wide-ass German car, with a bad motor. Well, you're not going into a parts house and finding engine parts for one of those. Al's father, Don Diego, came up from Colombia with his other son, Guillermo. Both of them were top-of-the-line machinists. They got some billets and made pistons. They took the cylinder head and rebuilt it. The Horch belonged to some San Francisco movie guy and when we started it up, it ran so smooth and so even, and the guy paid a big fat bill. I don't know how much, but you cannot get that kind of work done now for fifty times whatever he paid then.

I am now a single dad. For about three years up in North Beach I had a good life and so did my kid. That whole later addiction and crime stuff is a story that's been told so many times it's got hair on it. Fuck it. I did what I did, went to prison for it, and when I got out my life changed, and I did too.

Writing this now, I am way more inclined to write in stages as the memory appears, than I am to write about the sadness and sorrow and oft told tales of overdoses and death. Now a skinny old man, I can almost hear the Lone Ranger and "Let us return to those thrilling days of yesteryear" with a backing song by Fleetwood Mac: "Thunder only happens when it's raining."

There are some more stories, cars and people and places, motorcycle madness, risk after risk, dares and double dares I took. Lights out. The freeway at night. In and out of lanes, and that sweet line by Sweet William. *I have witnessed your defiance in your accelerations. A tailpipe symphony.* Fuck it. What are they going to do, send me to Vietnam?

Been there, done that. The green beret is on my bookshelf now, fifty-eight years later.

Sunlight streams through the glass door to my left. Here in Florida, twenty-two years into another century alive. Going back, almost like a patrol, into both the bright and dark past. I keep reading, and I can honestly say I read between three and five books a week, as I have since I was about eleven years old. You learn things, or at least you think about how this or that has affected you or had an effect on your life. This whole trope about knowledge or wisdom? Notches on the wooden stock of your carbine. Wrinkles on your skin and the creaks and groans of bones. You, me, everyone who gets the gift of growing old. That passion, that anger, that lust, all of those things that now seem like, "Well, it seemed like a good idea at the time." I do think, however, one of the things I have learned about myself is that I was wired backwards at the factory. Sort of like British cars that are wired negative earth, grounded reverse polarity. How some things just always came hard for me, like math, or something as simple as sitting still. Did I learn about attention deficit disorder? I did not have to; I was born that way. Any shiny thing, any sideways look, distractions, or noises called my name.

When I was about three or four years old, I had a bad eye. It rolled around in my socket and I was cross-eyed and clumsy. I got sent to my Aunt Celia's house on 47th Street and was going to get two operations at the NYC ear, eye, nose, and throat hospital. I had two cousins who were a bit older than me. Rose Louise and Geraldine, they were big girls, as was Aunt Celia. The dad, Uncle Tony, had lost a foot in WW2 and had a fake foot he kept in a shoe, and to this day I can remember him chasing me with that foot, and how I would howl, both a bit scared and a bit excited that I could go hide under the table. The two girls would each get a quarter from their dad. He had one of those change dispensers that he wore on his belt that made getting a quarter something more than if it had come out of his pocket. He owned five taxi cabs and drove one himself.

The family would send me across the street to Caspadora, an Italian deli and bakery, in the same store where Hile's Kitchen used to be, and apparently that's how Hell's Kitchen got its name. I would get a handful of penny candy, spumoni, caramel, and some of those cookies with chocolate tops. The sisters and I would sit together on the stoop. Did I mention that those girls were big? They ate well, and funny enough, I would try to keep back a few pieces of the candy in my pocket for later, but that never happened. I would wind up eating them all before we ever went inside.

Do I remember the operations? No. I do know I had to wear an eye patch, and Aunt Celia would let me have her big button box, and I would play pirate on the living room floor with the button box as my treasure chest.

My dad would sometimes drop by on his way to work at Rock Center. Sometimes he ate with us. Aunt Celia and my dad were fantastic cooks. Braciole, homemade ziti, and a sauce that was to die for. From the bakery across the street a loaf of bread that was still warm when we ate at the table. I sat there with my eye patch, feeling like a refugee. Again, in third or fourth grade my eye got all fucked up again. I had to get another operation and I had to wear glasses.

Those fucking glasses. I hated them. I lost them twice on purpose, and my dad got really mad at me. I remember him saying, "You've got to wear them until your lazy eye gets better or you're going to be a gimp." I went over to the yard three houses down and took them from the leaf pile where I had lost them on purpose. By fifth grade I no longer had to wear them. Then I lost them for good.

So that wired backwards part. That I would find out more at forty years old in AA about all that restlessness and irritability and discontent. Back in the 60's when I would smoke a lot of pot or hash, I reacted differently to the high than most people. Most people get sort of mellow and laid back. Me? Hyped up city. That was until the first time I hooted up a big rail of cocaine. It was as if the sky opened up and bells were ringing and everything was clear and I could see for miles. Calm, utterly calm, not fidgety, not chewing my fingernails, not getting up and sitting down and getting up again. Clarity pumping through the intricacy of brain waves. No feedback. No background noise. What I would give now to not have gone as far down as I did. But I also know it took what it took to get me to the bottom. I had to reach the bottom to stop digging.

Also, the jazz of it all, how in Vietnam I was never more alive than when I was being shot at and shooting back. I came out of Vietnam feeling almost like I felt when being chased by Uncle Tony and his fake foot. I ducked another scary deal. Never thinking about death. No, badass Green Berets don't think like that at all. Which is a lie. I thought about death a lot. But, putting on my boots, getting on that chopper, being the jazz, seeing how far I could go and then going further, saying to myself, "This shit ain't killed me yet."

I do not know. What I do know, is I do not act, think, or live now like I did then. Characters like Richie from the mafia, or Peter McKenna, no longer seem romantic or appealing to me; they somehow reflect that plunge into hedonism and predatory behavior that I now find troubling at best. I cannot say exactly how, not wanting to moralize or critically come off as better than, or more "enlightened." No, in the process of recovery, both 12 step and just getting older, seeing things that back then, seemed like fun, but became fully self-destructive, like being sort of ashamed not having any kind of formal education, but not doing what it would take to get one. YOU KNOW YOU GOT IT IF IT MAKES YOU FEEL GOOD. In passing you get this either nostalgic or lost days feeling, that leads me to sit quiet and recall all of the both good and bad times, mixed up in what my whole generation live with, lived by, and became who we are now, either by experience or by failure. I can now, so many years later, see that skyline vista, out that window on 5th St. I really can see it, night-fall lights, buildings full of glass stars. Roadway traffic creating rivers of movement, wondering sometimes where are they going, what are they thinking, as some stop at red lights and the river becomes an eddy of backed up cars. I am also in this book not going to be so time frame limited where I do not use the benefit of many years now of looking back, to make either reason, or understanding of some motive, action, or just plain heart break. I am not here to go on about the war in Vietnam and the first few years back, where I had no idea at all how both tortured and affected I was by what I had seen, (not so much done). I do now again, after many years of both study and some pretty extensive therapy, see how not giving a fuck about rules or laws or social order…

The mess today only last hours or maybe half a day. Not like the messes back when that went on for years, and now it is not what I think or feel, it is what I do. Then, I just kept doing stuff that made more mess. The equal of helpless or powerless to affect change, because of about the worst thing I can think of: "It seemed like a good idea at the time." Scheme and plot have both delusion and denial mixed up as coping strategy. On Friday, I mailed some copies of my new books to that *little sister* who told me, "You do not have to live like this anymore," with a note, "You believed in me when I could not believe in me. For that, love now an always."

Quite a few years after all this tale starts and ends, I had a boss in Oregon who knew me (or his oldest brother did) back when we were on our way to Vietnam. I worked for that man for 15 years. In a conversation we had, he reminded me that what was don't count, what is does. At least 3 of the managers in his then 8 dealerships had problems with me; he would move me, never get mad at me, just tell me, "How far you have come, I do not look at minor shit." This was about the time I fully restored for him a Pontiac Firebird, and he gave me a week tip at the most fancy resort in Oregon. Yeah, when I am writing this I think about the rewards some people gave themselves by just avoiding me, or shit can me outright.

    Living now, again by what I do, cause no harm to me or to anyone, because being trusted now means more to me than all the loot in some safe that I ain't about to go crack open. I worked one time over 6 hours on a floor safe that defied my usual tricks. The wind up was I got it out the floor and opened the bottom of it, just enough to pull out the money, and it was not much money.

    I get my monthly SS check now, and say a prayer when it hits the bank about let me live in my means and not care about what I might want, just be about what I need. I do have an over 40-year theory now, about easy come easy go. Working bent fingers over some pile-o-shit-box car, or service one of the best cars ever built, yeah, I earned that check. Probably why now when I look back as honest as I can, I did not have values because I did not value myself. I do now. I told somebody today I think more about keep my dog happy then I worry about me. Peace safety and length of days. I again question going back to 50+ years ago, when I like to think times were different. They were, but the underlie madness of our out-of-wack social order that I do sort of side-eye look at now; then it was not a concern, only not getting caught or wind up in a jackpot I could not talk my way out of or pay my lawyer to. Combine that with when you're young you think you're bullet proof, or like that, when you're old you do know better. I am finding it hard to believe today, I got to stay home more even then I want to, lest some jack-wad shit-head makes up their mind to spray bullets and don't even care who they hit…Not only am I not bullet proof, I ain't near as fast and strong as I used to be. I do sometimes cry to myself about the wasted days, and the way things just kept getting worse and I was as much spectator as I was the one doing that shit.

MANY A TEAR HAS TO FALL, BUT IT'S ALL A GAME

And all of that led to a kind of sadness I still feel sometimes now. Did I never feel a part of anything? Did I never feel good enough? There was always what felt like an ailment or malady chasing me down. I don't know.

What I do know now is about being powerless and being unable to manage my life. Like I said earlier, it was always about what I could get away with. Then I had a few years in a cell to contemplate the error of my ways.

The years are a bit clearer than the months. It was 1966. I had been back from Vietnam since March. In fact, it might have been early in 1967. My second cross-country run in the VW van with kilos of pot. My brother Tommy hooked me up with Richie from the Mafia. I was living with Patty Keen on 2nd Street near Avenue B. One of those apartments with the bathtub in the kitchen, with a cover so it doubles as a counter. Anyway, I had about eight or nine kilos left, and

Richie would come on a Monday and take some, then on Friday come and pay and take more, and so on and so forth. I had made a pretty good sum of money.

There was a building on 5th Street that was sold to another one of Richie's pals, and he wanted some people he knew to move in. I got the top back apartment on the 5th floor which was in pretty sad shape. I hired this guy Warren Brown and one of his buddies to go and clean it up, build a sleeping deck and re-do it. It was gonna take a month or so. In passing, I must mention the rent was $87 a month. I know people who now live in that building who pay $3,000 for the same apartment. Oh, yeah. Progress.

So, my brother and Abbie Hoffman come over and get eight ounces of pot; then they go out to Coney Island to my dad's house, sit at the kitchen table and roll up a few thousand joints. I don't even know what my dad thought of that. I did hear they brought my mom a case of beer, a bottle of Four Roses. They also brought a stack of about four hundred one-dollar bills.

Tommy was doing pin joints and running a card game on 16th Street at the time. He had some money. I can't remember if they paid me for the pot. What they did do, and it was in the papers, was go to Wall Street and dump all of those joints and dollar bills off a railing or something and watch the neckties swarm all over them. As far out as this is going to sound, Abbie was kind of a Jesus in his day, with books he had written such as *Revolution for the Hell of It* and *Steal This Book* bringing him a lot of fame. I did not know him all that well, but did know his wife Anita, and my Patty was sort of a political cause of her time in Mississippi as a freedom rider. She had a side hustle too. She would buy used overalls and cut the legs open and sew them up like a skirt. She sold as many as she could make. Revolution? Well, maybe not.

Tommy and Abbie, and I think a guy named Tree–who was pals with Owsley in California–had some LSD and put up this hoax that if you dry banana peels and smoke them they will get you high. You could not find a banana below 14th Street for weeks, and you could smell them cooking in ovens all over the Lower East Side. Walter Bowart, publisher of The East Village Other, put an image of a banana peel on the cover of one issue because of the hoax.

The apartment on 5th Street is done and we move in. I get on the phone to Arizona, and my buddy just got a big load of both the best Mexican ever and a hundred or so kilos of Panama Red. I drive out there and get a lot of it, go to Frisco and sell it to this longshoreman who had the nickname of Bugs. With that money, I go see Leo Sapeniza and get 101 Elsie Street. It was I guess what they now call a straw man deal, where MiMi and his son Ali Boy have the title, and Leo and his real estate company are the managers of the property. I never did figure out how all that was set up, but it would be later when it got sold, and I would not get the money till about ten years later. Had I got it in '76 or so, it would have gone up my nose.

There are so many of these memory holes, I am try to fill 'em as I can and go on each page as if that page were the one that could make the narrative flow. To the last page, and the both have and lose the house on Elsie St., not to say there were only bad times after that. A mix, just like everyone else's life has up down and sideways. Time, it is what any real effort or project takes to do right. It seems like I have covered the time from '66 to '76, but know there were many more events and places and people who need more both exposure and filling out. I also am very clear on not wanting to be digging a hole I cannot get out of, by what I think is another song line: "What's too painful to remember, we simply choose to forget." I got that part down. When some of the relationships were good for me but not so good for others. That entire 10 years I would steal anything I could, even before it became only to fuel my drug habit. Having read numerous books, both about Vietnam and the after effect of... PTSD? It seems I would never admit to that, only thinking that I got my ass shot at so some fat fuck could get richer, and I think that other part of not even knowing (or caring) about right or wrong, only about what it seemed like I could get away with. Without jumping too far forwards, to the sober years, and knowing "It seemed like a good idea at the time" was indeed something I needed to cure myself of. As it became more clear that I would never cure my addiction, only get that one day at a time reprieve based on maintain my spiritual condition. There will be pages on what I go on and on about the difference between spiritual and religious.

Do I believe in God? Or the sometimes divine nature of humans, who have the interface interactions and provide either moral, money, or indeed spiritual support. I had to learn things somehow in all that reading I have done, that a lot of people learn that stuff in grade school. I had to, I sometimes still have to, learn the hard way, by half intent and half result.

In time going by, finding out how things really work, at least things one can either fix or give up on. Much like it seems writing is, the thinking meets the blank page, it goes with some mix of "this fits, that does not," and every good mechanic knows when things be fitting. Take this class say on welding, or on engine assembly; there are both formulas and rules, the % of acetylene to oxygen, or the oil clearance on crankshaft bearings, you cannot fudge it or make it up. If you do, the metal burns, or the engine seizes up. In telling a tale of places and people, the formula seems to have a way wider area to work with. In all of this, however many pages, part of it all is to free me from angst and dark memories. Yesterday, I did a salute to *Howl*, the greatest minds of my generation and like that. Well, my take was bumboat wander back into, you bet, them dark days, when so many burn up flame out fall down and never get back up. Carol Thomas, a bartender and dope dealer, cat nip to women, and pretty healthy guy. In less than a year he looked like a waking skeleton. Dead as a rock face down, on his desk in that basement apartment, with a pile of not yet smoked-up free base. My ex-commanding officer was his roommate. He calls me and I went over; way past anything anybody could do. And at that time, I was involved with Carol's ex-wife, who was a big time coke whore herself. O that whole about 5 years of daily disasters. I would bet all I own had I started in on that free base, I would be long dead now. That I am alive, sober, and able to recall up the times that… given what? Angels, my own at that time hard as nails body, and, yeah, totally What?corrupted mind? I have no idea.

    I go now, way back, to when the whole idea of being an outlaw, a criminal, had the lure that being a gas pump jockey and helper at the gas station in the repair bay, didn't. Mob guys who bought shoes for more money than I made in a month. Thieves and thugs called good earners. The movie

A Bronx Tale, factor in later, looking back at Uncle Mi Mi, my cousin and the guys that hung around Neptune's Arms; who slip me a 20 here and there, let me wash their cars, and often sent me on errands, one time with a bag of money I dare not open or even look in. On the other side, Uncle Geno would sometimes put a fully counted collection of change in the ash tray or leave like some folded cash in the glove box, have me do a service or gas up the car then park it. While I am busy on the boat dock or with some other task, he'd go count every nickel. O, it would be about a few years later, after Vietnam, he would tell me about that, and later in my job as a foreman in a garage I would do the same thing then go look; if it was a dollar short, the guy was toast. Yeah, you steal shit at home is like shit in your food bowl. The intent here was a big part of my own growth, knowing "easy come easy go," and the weight of your own daily internal burden of shame.

No more, not now and thankfully not for a long time. My mistakes now are pop off my yap on Facebook over dumb shit. I might a cure myself o that too. We all yearn for acceptance and love, support and join in; the what AA calls the road to happy destiny. I am not now nor ever been all that keen on *happy*, but thankful, tranquil, even dare I say content. Add subject to pretty severe mood swings, but they do not last, and my own anger is so subsided now, I really only get mad at myself, no matter the, "You big dummy you dip shit you meat sack," etc etc, I have gotten into with some my way or no way fools. There is no one way; no, the part of being older and, so help me even just a bit more wise, you know it. Every freeway has lots of exits, that whole it is the journey not the destination thing. Not that long ago, two guys who

I knew well, both of them sober and had pretty good lives, killed themselves. That and that clap trap about the only existential question? Nah, I again look back over them pages here; the dark days and the life now.

    I do not want my life to end till I really feel like I both honor and show by my works how glad I am that I was pulled up pulled over and laid down the law, the *real law*, you get what you give, you earn your keep, and you (I) ask all who read this, all who helped me through the last few years to see I care about you and love it that you care about me. About 3 hours ago, I was driving on Green River Parkway, past the spot where I spun out and flipped over that Corvette and broke my neck. I pull over and I lie on my face. "Thank you God, let me not waste a day of this now," that I did not wind up dead, and my broken neck is not a problem now because I did what I was told, and other than some lung issue and some other pretty drastic weight loss I am about as good to go as good to go gets...Ever onward, even if I have written a lot of this only to let it go, be gone them demons who used to haunt me, I took them apart and found out what they thrived on. I don't give them a rusty nail now. I feed myself the parts of living that keep me alive.

    Let the dead bury the dead; yet linger on some of them who this whole book is mostly dedicated to, those who were there for me, the ones departed and the ones here. And you know what? Writing poems is one thing -- stack up a few lines to say what the feeling is. This is pages and pages of my life and times...into the both mystic and dead ass on the ground-wire circle of power and ideas.

    It is almost like the best boss I ever had who would complement me on a job, then say, "And what are you gonna do next?" He bought a Ferrari car, a yellow 308, and had it sent to the shop; came over and said to me, "Go over this one an tell me to keep it or sell it. I got it for a really good price."

I gave it the full 90 point inspect and drove it like 10 miles, went over to his office and told him, "Does not seem like it's been abused but it is a early version an the carbs need a bit more attention alla time en you are gonna wanna do."

Some guy shows up with a flatbed and tells me that he is going to take the Ferrari to this other guy. I see the boss getting in his car and call out, "Did you know it is going?"

He just laughs, walks over to me and says, "Don't *ever* let on that I do what you tell me to." We both had a good laugh.

OUT OF THE DARK I HEAR THEM CALLING (GOING TO PRISON SAVED MY LIFE)

Yeah, *On the Yard*, that whole time, is another story. All that happen before is this one: *101 Elsie St*. Years of both hedonism and sorrow. *Garage Tales* and *On the Yard*...it is hard for me thinking some one would believe how a guy could get out of prison and be both a big time Ferrari mechanic and radio personality, get sent back to Vietnam by CBS-TV, and some the other things in my later life...I got to Italy in '73 to train on the new mid-engine cars...I sure did. Did I go on a nosedive to crime and drugs and fall apart? All that happened. My other problem is to be clear on what was really going on and what I wish had never happened...
 in that...

I had a love affair with a woman name Nancy Anello. And it is too hard to write about or even want to…she was indeed the love of my life, "The lady who went to Asia." After we had moved in together on Precita St…and when she came back…"I came home to have your children and I love you too much to see you destroy yourself"…she rented a U-Haul, drove herself to NY, then moved to Bali and never came back. Or if she did, she never contacted me…and a few times I did look at her facebook page and the gallons of tears…

Yeah, to the other part in this. There are some stories about women that again people would find hard to believe. One of them was a 90-million dollar heiress who used to have me come over and service her, but told me, "If you ever say you love me or need me you won't come over here no more." What they say in AA is I did not have relationships; I took women hostage. But some of that is not true. There are 3 of them now who still love me and me them; we just do not see each other, but one of them did come down here for almost a month. And I say here, that was the end of my romantic life, and it was. Less talk about it and more in the pages of this.

OK. Prison is very much segregated, by tiers, by locations and activity on the yard. Different cliques and what is called *cars*. Who you hang with and who you share your commissary with is just about as clear a race divide as it is any place in America. Now on the yard, you walk with your road dogs, and I was able to avoid any gang stuff other than the biker group I was tag in. The Aryan brotherhood, the Black Gangs, the Mexican Mafia La Emie, and like that. There was a very clear pecking order, and when there was a potential flare up, or a real or imagined slight diss or outright, "That mother fucker ate his last meal," or like that, the big time shot callers, both black and white and the latinos (there were when I was there no major Asian tip), would sit by the basketball hoop and either work it out or let the combatants have their event. It did lead one year to over 200 days of full lock up, where you leave your cell once a day, for a walk the tier and shower once a week, all the food is carted in, and there is no movement outside of med calls or court dates.

Now, I mention Rebo and Ronny. OK. Had their lives been different, they both could have been olympic weightlifters. Rebo could bench press almost 700lbs and Ronny could do 3 reps with 450. They would spot each other and there was never a word said about white or black. Most all of us would watch, back a bit, and see those two push 1500lbs of iron like it was cupcakes or kids toys. One time I asked Ronny about all that. "Why not have Lep and I spot you?"

He said, "I do, when the weight is something you two could lift off me. But if I got 500 or more on the bar, I want Rebo who could snatch it off me and not even break a sweat." Same went for Rebo, I think. Then you get to, they did not *talk*, they were not buddies or any of that. I had a bit of a problem because there were three black guys I knew from the street, and one's brother was my best fishing partner. I asked Ronny how I could kick them down some of my commissary and he told me, "I will look into that."

He went to another shot caller and asked him. The guy told him to have me put it on the bench near the basketball court and he would see the right guys got it. I only did it once, but in the library I did teach some black guys how to read. Funny enough, the library was off limits to any kind of brag buster bullshit. Jail house lawyers and other on the books guys like me were not at all about any of that any how. I might have said already one of them guys got out and named his daughter Dominique after me. I had a very extensive education in prison, both con wise learn and book study. That other part mentioned about learning to live.

In, I think, about 15 or so years in my post-Vietnam life, I was, by intent or by default, a mix of some productive time and some big waste. In this book, that now, reading as I go, both scatter and move from place to place and hearing in my mind the phrase, "No matter where you go there you are." Sudden takes, some disaster moves, and some just by happenstance or blind luck I got by. We, the lot of us, this entire human species, have all our own ways of either remembering or being reminded by our stations in class or in life, how or if we fit in.

Adjusting the flame. A best way to say, is with a gas torch a very bright yellow small start and an even brighter blue, will weld or cut most metal. I see that in my mind's eye as how you adjust things in time and space, people and place. In some parts re-read, and go on, how for machines and bikes and cars and like that, there was never any mean or uncaring part. In person relations, yeah, what is in it for me. I hate that, and it has been another part of big adjustment to how who what and where I have become what I am now. A bit of a mess sometimes over the oldest if I only had, pffft, I am not ever now gonna be all bound up in that. My scars and my sorrows are the proof of surviving past the bad days. I have seen this now over 30 years with cases more dramatic and torn up than mine who moved on got over it and became a good friend or someone who could be ok in their own skin, as I hope I am now.

I am going to go back here to about 12 years old. And I am not about to go on about my mom who drank too much or my dad who was, as I see it now, overwhelmed with just keeping us fed and housed. I had the chances to learn, and it was one thing my dad did tell me, about learning how to learn. I took things apart and put them back together again. I would indeed wind up most of my later life doing that for money and for the love of understanding how things work. To, at this age, finally able to see what I can and cannot do about the political the religious the class the places and times we are all in now.

To go from working and being employed to employ myself as the keeper and adjuster of the flame. That flame that is inside us, the hard parts about from brain to heart and heart to brain. Dare I say about the best laid plans of mice and men. I have for the last few months done more yard-work and planting flowers and small bushes than I have since my 20 years in Oregon as a grounds keeper. It is like the balm of life, careful plot place and care for what becomes the daily view, as I sit and think about how and why this entire book is as much about what I saw said and did, as what I see do and say.

It takes a lot to laugh but it takes a train to cry. In almost all the times I write there are song lines and some movie parts that enter into my back beat, or add to how or what I want to say. I have been taking some notes, and finding out that the purpose of a memoir is as much to let it go as to let it flow. In what now is the springtime of my 77th year bouncing around life, from here and there. I have to say, the last 8 years or so have been very stable, other than the month-to-month money drama. See, just like now I can hear Willy and living in the promised land. I have collected things, some I wonder how ever did I manage to keep; I have some small bears that Nancy gave me in 1979, panda bears. I also have three Navajo bears, one big black one, and one turquoise one with a baby bear up an iron wood tree. We got that in Arizona in 1980. I have about 10 fishing reels I have had for that long too. I think sometimes about other things: books, fishing gear, cars, motorcycles, bicycles, even some old clothes that are long gone.

Take it all in, put it all out; where working this really helps me see it was not all tragic or all sad or did not have some genuine humor and fun. It did. One thing I can easily see is how much I've been all my life in one kind of mood swing or another. The fact that I even mention Nancy, that I was sort of told it might be better if I leave all that out. There are, I bet you, way too many books and stories about love lost. It was the last time we had any communication between us. In Oregon when I got the job on the radio, and learned how to email. I sent her one. Told her about my new job, and how much it was then seeming like a really good fit. She did answer, best I can word for word, "I am glad you found something."

If I had 5 dollars for every time I was told, "You gotta write a book," I'd be fat bank happy. In my golden years (laugh track), going over note books, memories, people places and things. So funny as it might sound, some of those *things* I remember better than people or places. Bags of dope, motorcycles, cars, tools, stalls and benches in about 20 garages I worked in. I often question the *purpose* of memoir type work. It is ego? Is it going away, not saying farewell, not leaving a trace behind? Another thing that happens just like that last line, songs of them days, and ear worms now, "Hank why do you drink why do you roll smoke why must you live out all the songs you wrote." To some quiet moments, when sappy as I am, *Moon River* or *Some Enchanted Evening* just plays a back song to my fingers as I type. That too, I have about 75 notebooks, all filled up…about 15 of them, I toy with the idea of burning them before anyone ever sees them, pity pot bullshit by the pages full, and in honesty, I did more blame myself than I did people places or things.

So, *101 Elsie St*. Why? How many of us the age I am now, and gone back over the (another subtitle) of our own lives? I have read or know of about 50 books that were written about and after Vietnam. I wrote two of them myself. So, with this lingering thread in my head about *Then N Now*, some days the memories come up bubble up quick like, other times it is a few days of "what really did happen vs what I wish had." The why? Well, I saw that house in mid-63 on my way to my own adventures in Asia, and somehow like an icon like a talisman like a mental keep sake, "That house is gonna be mine." And how can you say some 6 years later *it was*. To that other part about writing about yourself, to me it is better when I can be a part of time, be a friend, lover, and, yeah, sometimes a total asshole; that part of the healing now isn't self-blame or any of that, to really dig deep, into both my childhood and that war and those drugs and that crime, that too often now is some stereotypical look at VN vets, and to say this "with tears" of all those who kill themselves. I have taken this time and this effort to be as clear and in at least some measure of timeline order. However, it is again as moods and memories come, the ideas of make it expand the lives and places and not just be my own life story.

WHAT A LONG STRANGE TRIP IT'S BEEN

The writing life, or writing about life, yours, mine too, with that over used phrase *the passage of time*...in the present, it seems hard to alter or romance or slant it to be what you want it to, as (o I hate the phrase) it is what it is. Then lets go back, say about 52 or so years. I have my one-year-old baby girl on my lap, and we have this animated conversation about the front stairs on Elsie St. "You could fall off an bust ya noggin," and at a year old, she is not exactly multi-verbal, but gives me a look and laugh, like, "What? I got hell a balance." Or whatever her giggler reply really. We are going to go out, and climb up those stairs. Her mom is less than happy about that. The oft used "she is not yr trained bear," but in my heart she sure is; in fact, my name for her then was Marme coco bearme. Beautiful Frisco day, you can see most all the city from the front yard. She starts up the stairs and there is a banister that I had sanded down and stained;

she gets to the first turn, and looks down at me, and *leaps* down into my arms. I like to feint, thinking if I missed, her mom would kill me. She wants to do that again. Laughing, she does; then I go to the bottom step, she jumps from about 6 steps up and I hold her up over my head (that photo is somewhere). Then we sit on my old easy chair in the front yard and I tell her about careful and safe. She falls asleep on my lap. If I look back, if I really think hard about it all, those first 4 years of her life were the best times in mine. I can feel her, yeah, 52 years later, snuggle up there, and smell her baby sweetness. I sat there with her, and never even dreamed that it would all fall apart, that her mom and her would leave me. Not that they did not have good reason to. That day is etched in my cells.

I spoke to her this AM and told her, "I think about you sometimes, when you were very little," and her reply was joy in my soul. "I know dad. I feel the same about my baby girl (who is going on 12 now) as you did about me."

After they left, I would stay on Elsie St. for about 2 more years as my life started to come apart, not all that fast, but in a steady downhill cycle, that would end up in my going to prison. There were some days, just sit in my cell and remember Elsie St. and them days when it did look like I was over Vietnam, and I would be a family man.

And the fact, that from about 13 to 19 my daughter and I were not in much contact at all is, indeed like death is pain of heart. Well, since she was 20-some and I was 40 and my life took a big uphill turn, all for the better, we talk all the time; in fact, go ahead laugh, yesterday my dog started to bark, the UPS guy shows up, with 3 boxes of Grandpa Pine Tar Soap. Between us, that old joke about, "Dad, you stink," from when I always did smell like gasoline or gear oil. Yup. I call her, thank her for the soap and say, "Soon as I off the phone I gonna go shower." And the laugh she gave me is back to those giggles all that long ago.

    I sit for about half an hour, looking out at my back yard. The big rose bush, the flowering Frangipani tree, my vines and, over the fence, the preserve trees and wild space. I never had a spot like this that some disaster of my own making wouldn't make it go poof and wind up, like I did for years, moving *again*. It takes this part of my mind soul and heart, to look back and be brutally honest about it, no gild on the lily or oil on the lens. How bad was it? I did not even know I hated myself, had issues that all these years later, I have heard a 100 or more people in recovery tell me they had the same issues. The various bottoms all dope addicts and drunks hit. I was just on the phone with Ed, one my oldest friends, and we both broke up when I remind him of what he and Carlos both said about my last book: "It would a been even better if I did not know you." Said with both humor and love.

    It was Ed who said long ago, "If you don't get some help I gonna have to shit can you." Yup, he did. So, it is some time in like '75 or '6, it is 3am, I am in an alley off Broadway tore up from the floor up, sniffing up the last few hits of the bitter narcotic poison, I hear the traffic, an see the now muted neon, reflected in the mud puddle I just about lie down in. I have found some of my notebooks from those days. O Dear God...

    In transpose correct and keep this as tight as I am able, I hear this other old line of mine:

> *Dominic such a beautiful line how*
> *much longer can this go on*

That line is in one of the notebooks I got back after getting out of prison. I have a box full of them. I can hear voices, I really can, of people who are not alive anymore; often times they remind me of things they did say while alive and we were together. One of them, my dear pal Spain the now gone artist, would tell me, "It is all about the work, not about the thinking or the reason. It is how the end comes and what is left is what was you and your value." I can hear that sometimes, even when he would call me penis wrinkle and I would call him fuck bubble.

I have heard in AA meetings a lot of times "It took what it took" to get here; and find out the, both, cause and reasons for the similar and not the difference between us. Old songs, old TV shows and some other random thoughts, about 40 or so of them, I just might figure out what this whole getting older and looking back a lot thing is all about. Partly, I think (cause really you never know), complex or motivational (muse) amuse, sad, sorry about some things and glad for some others gets mixed up and tied up in old songs, memories of things that happened a lot of years ago that are in your mind more real than what is afoot now. *Born in the sound of the outward bound and yearn to wander.* It is like, yeah, but I am home now, mixing up a bit of bored at the same streets and places, but knowing the mystery of somewhere else is just that. No reason to solve it, because if you lived in, say, 5 cities over a period of 60+ years, and even been across the world, it takes all that getting used to…that now, again about the getting older…is this just me or does everyone do this kind of reflections and maybe stuff? So, try to put the past in some kind of order, this happened and then that did, or had that not happened would all this look different now?

Towards the time my life really started to unravel, I could not keep a job for but a few months, an hour. A knight with out armor in a savage land. The Naked City? My own past, and now present, ways of record and remember with both a bit of sorrow and some really fond stuff about all those here and all those gone. Departed not gone.

There are, as I understand it, some rules and some theory about how you digest and live with past default behavior. That entire trope of unravel your own ball of yarn and knit a new sweater out of it. Not a lot of some things that did happen, as versus some I wish had, does change any of the real place space and time events. How any other lives came and went, as someone just in passing became someone who would help you change your own life. That has happened to me, and there are not enough pages empty left to list thank and honor them all. Some by only a comment they made in a meeting, and it was just what I needed to hear.

When I call my dog, she comes to me. Clear eyes and wagging tail. I've been buried in bleak and a mix of memories, old bad habits, old stinking thinking, and here and now I am not. Opened up a passageway into the better parts of the last 30+ years, from 40 to now. I did the work, I really did. I been to so many step meetings, I can do by rote most all the short versions of the 12x12. In the long version of the 4th step, "of relations we had not a clue," self-centered and selfish, suffering from a thousand kinds of fear. Well, not long ago, weeks in fact, I got a dose of fear that just about blew my doors off. "You very well might have drowned in your sleep." Holy hopping hamburger buns. Health? You know what? I've already mentioned Leo Sapenzia; at just about the age I am now he was at the Optimo Cigar Store on Mission and 29th St, playing the pin ball machine, and he told me (I was in my late 20s), "Ya health…I cannot get a hard-on, I cannot enjoy a steak dinner, you got ya health you got it all; you just got to stop being stupid." Man if I had only heeded that. My own take was I was bullet proof, invincible drama and dreams of the outlaw life. Yeah, fat lot of good that did me. I refuse to even say, "If I had it all to do over." Or worse, to fall into any of that *o poor me* bullshit. When Leo got me Elsie St, that was a big step up.

IT'S NOT SOMETHING YOU GET OVER

I had never really owned anything, I used things, I stole them, I swapped them; I had only one little toolbox but by the late '70s I had 90-thousand $ worth of tools. More than half of them are in my garage now. There is even a small hammer. I left it on a leaf spring, and it fell off on the road; on the way back, I saw it and stop and get it. There is not a time I have used that hammer since and not remembered that. One time while I was in therapy that woman came to my shop and looked over my tools and told me, "You're not near as crazy as you think you are." Nick Torelli used to tell me my tools were "the product of an organized mind." You know what, I spent most all of a year as the shop monkey cleaning his and Alfredo's tools. My own collection grew, and I have a toolbox now I have had since 1972. I have a German cart, called an Assistant. I call it my Cadillac. I once flew it to LA and re-built a 6-cylinder Fiat motor with just the tools in that cart, minus the machine work. Towards the time where I was really a very high paid and good mechanic. Then I got the job on the radio as the hi-way helper. And would go to some of my old garages and they give me the hi-five and "Mr. Big Shot."

There are pages here that bounce from time and place to other times and places. That is how my memory works; I can have a whole notebook full of ideas but can only really write about half of them in whatever order I think of them. It is like the time you find out who you are because of what you did or where you were; reflections in fog memories events people places and things, discovering who what and why you are. OK, people born and raised in New York City, I think, have an uncommon sense of either themselves or their place in the social order. Loud, almost to a person, spewing more opinions than Carter got little liver pills. The simple fact that almost all broadcast big time media was born there, too. You gotta be old to remember when there was only NBC CBS ABC and the outlying areas that got sub-stations and fed a daily dose of ticker tape news feed.

It is partly how, never even knowing, even suspecting, how damaged, morally, mentally, spiritually, I was. I never thought about who or what was responsible for the war, for the damage; again, just living that *if it feels good do it*, and care not about the moral and spiritual damage. Had you told me in say 1966, there were both teachings and ways to heal and become of value to yourself and others, I would've laughed at you. And looking back, some people did tell me things like that, those who were embracing the higher concepts of counterculture, both values and ideas, not just turn on tune in drop out. Not that any of this is an excuse or a plea about o I just did not know better. No, I really did not like who and what I became. Do I just revert here and go third person, as if someone else was doing the things I now dread having done? I have no clear answer for that, and I also know way better in my 70s than I did in my 20s and 30s. Despite some of the amazing people places and things, I was so lost and so angry, so without anything resembling either contrition or aware of how bad I hurt myself and others. Blind to anything but more drugs more money more crime and being on the edge all the time. And like in my last book, talking about want to be Ward Cleaver or some other television guy. I think here also I did know how to handle crisis and crazy but not a clue how to live life on life's terms.

How many people ask themselves, "What if it had been different?" Life? Time? Spaces? Places?. Parents, siblings, people who lived on your block? I says a lot, when someone (me any one) tries to record passing years, all that time place things. I bet my shoes anyone who writes, or tries to write, gets bogged down in the maybe of it all. What did happen, what so hard to accept some things that did not happen, you can only muse about. If she had said yes, instead of, "You got to be kidding me," and like that. When I was young, like 10 or so, it would just kill me, even if I did not know it then just felt left out, or dare I say deprived. Some kids' dads could build things; one kid had this roller skate scooter that was all doweled and jointed, with a swivel front end that could turn. What we had were old 2x4s with a wood box and wore out your sneakers rub along to keep it going, those noisy old metal skate wheels, and so what, we had fun. I can look back and see how some of those things were, yes, very painful. But you don't really know it then, and that kid with the fancy scooter? Nobody liked him anyhow. Part of my own both desire an ambition to record, reflect too, on wise guys, hop heads, gypsy princesses, early puberty Jewish girls, Italian an Irish guys I grew up with, and was half of each of them by blood and by choice...

Because that whole deal about tomorrow is a maybe you could indeed, as another friend of mine did this week, wake up dead. And be no more; into that other real mystery to me about the end or the next great movie life play stage or sideline you get to be on, seen or not. Who knows...

I am now back on that motorcycle, my ass is sore, and my hands are vibrating from the bounce in the front end, and wherever it was I got to, there I was, to have to get some gas, adjust my seat, and go back to where it was I came from. Why? Because that is what this whole lurid saga is about: I got away with I got caught with I did this I did that. And now I just sit around and think about it. Because I break some bones now, I'm going to be bent and broken alright; most dangerous thing I do now is dream and speculate about it. I am safe, you I hope are safe too. I got whatever time I get now to make what was broken and sad re-made, with word salads of adventure, war, crime and love. And I tell you this from my heart, I been loved way more than I ever thought I deserved to be and now I just try to love back the most and best I can. Page by babble brook page, line them up, line them down, put them in the printer and in your hands...and I tell you my life ain't no more important than anyone's. I just got the chance and place to write mine down...

Since it seems to me this whole effort is a prose version of my poetry book *Then N Now*, I've sure been going on about then, how about some now. In 2005 I moved to

Florida, partly because I got a job offer, partly because both my brothers were there (they both have since passed on). I was offered by Mercedes Benz a roadside job, being that I am a guild tech with that outfit. 5 years of out of gas, flat tire, dead battery, or a no start that needed a tow. It was a wonderful way to learn my area. I had parts of 3 counties, north south and west, can't go very far east, but did a lot of work on the barrier islands. I met some amazing people, even 2 of them who knew my dad, and another one who knew me.

This is a riot. I get paged to go to this woman's house; her car won't start. I show up, a guy comes out the house, you could not make this up if you tried. "What? You steal cars now legally?" It was a cop who was a partner of my cousin in Coney Island and it was my cousin who busted me for stealing cars at 15 years old. I just cracked up, put a new battery in the car and it was out of warranty, but I give him a 50% discount on the price. We shake hands and he asks me about my cousin. Hard tale there. I told him he got busted in some dope deal and just sort of went away. Not to jail, but to wherever. He knew a bit about it and said a lot of guys fell to that money that was so easy to get.

Another one, a woman whose dad owned a jewelry store in Rock Center and remembered as a kid my dad and his big voice. The other was a former camera man for NBC who knew Patsy, and said, "Everybody knew Patsy."

So, now I've been very active in AA since I got here; met and married a woman, who on both sides of it was just better we parted and stay friends than wind up bitter and have some nasty divorce. I walked away and, yeah, we are still friends. Meantime, I had had enough of 2am flat tires on the Turnpike in the rain; enough is enough, I am 68 years old. I turn in my wagon and my keys and beeper and leave under mixed terms. They said I should have given them a month to train someone else.

The guy who owns the Snook Nook tackle shop told me, "Go upstairs and fix reels. I'll give you half the labor." I stutter about what I know about reels is what I know about mine. He laughs, "If you can overhaul one them fancy-ass motors, you can fix reels." 9 years I did that, and I loved it. Easy work and great connections for guys who would take me offshore and guys who would tip me pretty good too. The 2016 election put a stop to that. It was punch someone or just leave. I did. They called me back in a couple of months, but it was pretty clear my ideas about how a country should be run and theirs was 180 out. I left again and would not go back for anything.

Jump around Dom, yeah, I am.

OK that easy divorce, that "O dear where I gonna live now." I had a small warehouse where I kept a bunch of stuff; it was cheap and a bit dirty. I figure till something better came up, I will live there. O, about not training anyone else on that Mercedes job. Joey, who is like an adopted son to me, I took him out least 5 times and the few days I did not come in he did the roadside. He was very sharp and had good hands; got his Master Tech status, that doubled his pay. I call him and ask him to come help me move my tools. We show up at that hovel and he goes, "Wat da fk is this?"

Best I can do right now. "Bullshit," he says, "Come with me."

We drive over to the house he grew up in, his parents had both passed away and he let his sister-in-law live there, she was in all kinds of trouble and wound up doing a couple years locked up. The house was a mess, holes in the walls, dirty, the pool looked like it was where they filmed *The Creature from the Black Lagoon*. He says you can live here free for a year, fix it up, clean it up and we will see.

BUT IT'S YOU GET THROUGH

Going over old notebooks and other writing from the times in this book. How much the narrative has changed with this age I am now. If there is a saving part, I never ever tried to paint myself a victim of a mess I made, my own blame shame and guilt game overcame all of that. One more song line about *Wasted days an wasted nights*. It just did not seem then I would or could outgrow, get over or get out of my own way, enough to see a better life and way to live it. I might add at the present day, with a big part of this nation an armed camp, and the overcrowded areas, desperation not of one's own making, but of circumstances, both finance and political... How it seemed then? Anything was possible, that leads to a hand full of my own resentment, that I never did get smart about money, or get more concerned about, dare I say, old age. Even writing that last sentence I know full well, beyond my monthly drama bills, and keeping myself housed and fed, the very facts of others, weigh on me. When that group of bums lived near the Jensen Beach bridge, I used to bring them food, never once lecture or even act like I was better than,,no, not ever. In my own heart I knew I was reaching out, because I knew and fully believed that without my support and help group, I very well could have been living there too. The county cleaned all that up, it is not germane to the tourist industry or the snow birds to see the homeless, no, the illusion of a tropical paradise, in effect, with the local economy depending on for about 6 months a year that inflow of out of state out of country money. It does not change for me, and getting by is good enough, no matter the wail of it all: o dear, I am never gonna have my own fancy car, or my own this that or the other. When all I do have is more than I ever had before.

    Not so much things, but feeling and accepting my state of my state. O, how I go by the lottery stand at the market, and just laugh to myself about spending money I do not have to get money I am not gonna get. Ha, then I think you cannot win if you don't play. Who is deserving? I think that is a theme that runs through this whole book, when if I am fully honest, paying attention to the possible futures was never a concern. With just 3 of the cars I had and sold for minor profit, if I had them now, yeah, a lottery win just about. One of them, a 1500 Fiat Convertible, very clean and in good working order that I paid $400 for and sold for 1200, just went at the auction for 125K.

    None of that matters. I keep what I have in the best shape I can and continue to think that enough is enough, even more than I deserve. That alone, nag me, gag me, stop that shit now and 'ever. I do not suffer from trauma or unable to see past the kid I was or the times that were listed here, over and over. I do have to say in the now, looking back, what I thought was fun or adventures or just anything other than what was was; it is not now. I would never take the chances with my life I did then. Even if just yesterday, by about 300 feet, I was able to avoid a 5-car pile-up in, of all places, the parking lot of my local Publix market. I had to drive about 2 miles or so to get back home from that lot that is less than 1/2 mile from my house, all the time thinking how close that was; had I not stopped for someone crossing with their shopping cart I would have been in that wreck. I wrote a small poem about it and my dear JJ said, "Move to the country an paint ya mail box blue." That had me just yup; my other buddy said stay home stay safe. I think here about all the years where food or shopping was get it where and when you could. I bet I ate 90 to 150 meals at the Chat And Chew Cafe. Even when I moved to North Beach as a single dad, Mary and I ate out as much as we did home. That got better, however, with the love of someone who would come over and cook, and that in fact was where I learned to cook. Now days, I do cook, and every meal is a solid victory over dumb living and bad nutrition. *But sometimes you just might find you get what you need.*

    Clearly, all the hopes, wishes, dreams, predictions, ain't worth a pot o' beans. All that who are we? Why are we here? What happens next after you croak? All that is a pile of comic books shredded and tossed in the compost pile. Who knows? Well, I just told someone that it took a whole lot of years for me to be ok in my skin and get over my stupid. That, well, I might still have a reserve supply of stupid, but I try double hard not to act it out or sound like some jitter bug hop head nincompoop. Old Willy Nelson song about "living in the promised land," I get a big hit out of that some mornings when the light and the greens side is going from a bit of shadow to a glory of growing vines. Go back? go forward? sit still and wait and see? Yeah, if I have one really serious lament, it is not being strong, nimble and have some of the things I could once do easy, now be too hard to do. I looked in the garage this morning, putting away the laundry, and my old big red tool box, my Cadillac, even when I was strong, it took 3 or 4 guys to load it in my truck. There are about 50-thousand $ of tools, and every one of them has a memory attached. There is one 11mm wrench I heated up and bent to reach under the bottom bolts on a Maserati manifold; a collection of measuring devices, a rail of sockets from 6mm to 36mm, man alive.

The things I used to worry about that never happened and the things I did not pay attention to, like the ones got me a nice stay behind the walls. Back to predictions (laugh track inserted), how in who's name or what supreme being, could have told me my big drama now is my roof is too old for me to have hurricane insurance on this house. After Elsie St, I owned 3 more houses that really belonged to who I was married to, and I never really gave a toss about owning them. This one? well I don't own it either. I just want to live here till I die, and the deal is set up that my partner and my daughter really own it and get to either sell it or keep it or rent it out or whatever they want to do when I am no longer a factor in it. So after 4 full years of payments, what I built up in equity is gonna put a new roof and solar panels, cut the monthly electric bill by 75%. I bet my SS check, without ever lay odds on if this month is gonna have a bit left over or end of the month on rice and beans. So what? Living here and be able to write work think sit still play with my dog, the value is more than the cost, I tell you that.

Then somehow, out of all the other mish-mash of slip slide stagger and mumble about expenses, my computer is about to shit the bed. My buddy says for $500 he bring me a LINUS (da fk dat is?), and I be faster and more easy on the merry go round that is WWW or any of that. O well, I have re-read some of the old days writing here and seen where they *ain't gonna cook me eat me or send me in the jungle, no less put my ass in jail.*

What I have on my mind now is really only peace safety and length of days. The rest? More caddy wamp silly stomp semi-trailer loads of utter bullshit sold as conservative vs progressive and not any of that is gonna put a bit of chow in my belly. No less give the dog a bone. Sappy? Sad? Melancholy? Sometimes. Hopeful wishing sometimes. As days go by, in what an hour from now is a full home inspection and a pain in my tooshie about insurance an living by the law of the land. If you don't pay now, you're going to pay more later...what a fucking trap. Dollar for dime, the things I really care about don't cost x y or z. They are the things inside you that keep you off the grinding wheel or the lathe trying to make something square round or something round square. Step back, look at what you want, shape size and function, grind off the chaff and get the shape size and need, not want; it all goes round and round, and *it comes out here.*

A bit more about my reasons, my thinking, and how or why, recording writing and sort of explaining both the good and bad in 76 years of being alive. Almost odd to me is the way in some of my back pages life was way less stressful or worrisome. That said, any one this far in can see, I had made some bad choices and did some things that if not got me killed, sure did get me locked up. I hold on to that deeply now, had I not got put in prison I am sure I would not have lived 3 more years. No, free base and crack? Yeah, I reach out here to *Howl*, and add, "I saw some of the toughest bad ass bikers criminals an all round mugs thugs an like that, loose 100lbs an become empty bodies with a fire on they soul that cooked em cast em into outer darkness an left em so weak, they did not even cast a shadow, an I went a saw 2 of em put in a urn that was smaller en a pickle jar."

Yeah, that and the times of some slick ass dealers with money counting machines and cops on their payroll, all of that. I am standing in my stall at the Ferrari dealer on Green St in Frisco, and this guy and the then general manger are handing each other those over the shoulder man purses and who had the money who had the dope? No matter, I knew what was going on. Later on, in prison I met up with a guy who lived in Felton, a sub-area of Santa Cruz, and he knew those 2 guys also; told me he got 50K in dope fronted to him, and made 30K on the deal, then a bit after that, after one of the 2 been busted, he went up to Frisco and met this guy who said he was keeping the biz going and it was an undercover cop. Guy got 15 years when (and this is true) he bought a pound of coke from the cop and did not get 10 blocks away and was pulled over and busted. He told me they did that with that same pound of coke about 5 times. O man, a bit of the big time that was not me at all.

I look now at my daily life and think to myself just about every morning, I got my how many new chances and today the choices are about being better, more of service and less of self-serving, less of what I want and more of what I need.

Then I get to the parts about daily looking round online and *Brittany shakes her epic butt*. To the other parts of who shot who and never even find out why. I got such a case of the heebie-jeebies about daily news and fake information that I run to my own refuge of *know the truth be safe and do not start no shit*.

I took this book on to, in stages, list in stages, be forgiven in stages, explain the changes and hope on my whole soul someone else in the deep of it sees the way out from the bottom is to stop digging that hole and wait for the love and protection of others and the higher power chosen to lift up out of, and then put all that misery back in, that hole and bury it every day with notes and, yeah, pages, as a grave to your own dumbness and a headstone says **NO MORE**. Not today, that's for sure…o bless it all, deeply…Life with friends and teachers, men and women who give me a reason to be part of and not an isolated hoarse voice calling out when will, how will this end.

Speaking of holes in memory, and various events, I did have 2 Harley Davidson Sporters. One brand new with about 5000 miles on it, I left in Arizona, the other was a used one I soup up and trade for a BMW R-69s that I drove to California from NYC, and gave it to a guy for a new motor on a VW bus, just like the first one.

Going back and forward at the same time, I think or want the narrative as complete as I can make it.

The editing and the syntax…all that, my voice is me, but I have on purpose left out dese dem an dose, a lot of Brooklynese; the task was to write clear and express fully the sort of sub-title of *Out Of The Dark Into The Light*. I do re-read, a lot, both my work and others, clarity and tone, pace and not gloss over or exalt the bad, or overdo the good. In this now time, I do find it a bit unsettling in some of the days that were so dark. And the parts about my baby girl on Elsie St, that has now grown to a deep and fully loving relationship between me and her. That other part about support and carry me, till I could carry myself. Every effort here is about one life, in the times of many lives crossing. I do sit sometime and just glow, about who is still here and even more about the debt I owe to those departed who were there for me, even when I was not there for me. I cannot even list them all; those here, they know, those not, I hope in my soul they do too. Spain once told me, "The parts after you're dead might or might not go on. Live it now do the best you can."

My take on clean-up and correcting my typos and misspelling? Yeah, but I don't want this in the laundry. No, wash it up in the sink, wipe it off with a dish rag, and let me again re-read it and fist pump. How do I go on is part of it and the last pages are the first ones too, in the mix of how many years how many places faces and lives.

O Bobby Dylan, *we all got to serve someone*. Cap that with I take you all on a walk by Gravesend Bay, and some kid outta Coney Island wants to love you and have you love me. I lay down another lick here, from Elaine Paige, trying everything new, *they were illusions not the solutions they promised to be*. Some worked and some got me locked up. As of now, the only thing keeping me back is my own fear of overdo or underdo it all. Twisting in the night, abandon all fears and fly deep high and with my own voice even if sometimes the babble and scat takes a few looks…my time is all your time too.

In November of '85, a half month before I turn 40, I left Frisco with only 3 things at that point that really matter. Stay off dope, stop lie and steal, stay employed. I had not a clue about Oregon or the Church I was to be adopted into. I did really good on 2 outta 3 but telling lies was sort of my default mode, about either what I did or did not do, where I went or did not go. Simple as it is, it took some men/women in AA to teach me about partially honest is only partially sober. The manufactured truth never holds up because X hears Y and Z hears W, and when they compare notes, you're busted. That, just like staying employed, was a process.

My own deep anger and what they now call PTSD, and bosses and service managers were my other big problems. I did not even know a default mode, was a shadow-making part of how I did cope in my early life. Lies about my mother and her alcoholism; anything to keep what I knew to be not good enough thinking, was my escape clause. I have for the most part like 90% gotten over that. I lost my last wife over lies about money. I did.

Back now to finding Oregon and finding me. I met and married someone there who, to this day, I love and she loves me. It was not lies that drove us apart, it was my own not wanting to be grandpa at 60 to her daughter's kids. And there was the fact that she managed our money, and I had way more than I ever thought I did.

In the 20 years there I did not commit a crime. One time stands out. I was doing extra work for a used car place, and they had a week where they had between 20 and 50 grand in the safe. I knew it, and I could have peeled that safe the way someone else can open a tuna fish can. I told the priest, as I agonized about not clipping that loot. "It will lead you back down a road you have told me numerous times you do not want to be on."

I did not start to cry but I wanted to. "But I know I will not get caught."

That made him laugh. Then he told me, "How many times have you said to me, 'But I know what is real now'." That got him up from behind his desk and a hug. "The progress is what counts; the murmur of demons is real too you know."

It would happen as I live and breathe someone else broke in and took that money. The guy who owned the place and I were out fishing when it happened that Sunday afternoon. He knew who did it, and then comes to me and says, "I want you to go get me that money back."

I just about fell on the floor, and told him, "I had eyes for that money myself, an that guy I can bet you has already shot most of it on dope an hookers."

It would turn out the cops got him and he had about 18 grand left of what was 32K but the court made him a deal, a suspended prison time for full pay back. I often thought about the way I could have got to him sooner and lied about how much was there etc etc, but that too...

I had this great talk with my sponsor about all that. He was an old armed robber himself, did a long jolt in prison, and he gave me a cuff in back of my head. "Crime don't pay fuck ball. If you don't know that by now I might just have to throw you a beating." We both laughed.

20 years later, in '05, I would leave Oregon for Florida, with the same 3 ideas in mind, and other than my divorce here, already mentioned, I have not either done or got caught

doing anything that would wind me back up in stir. The pages already here, and the times on Elsie St and further into my utter life turn to hammered dog shit. Not any of that is about today or the last 16 years down here in the tropic zone, that I for the good times I call it, *Living in the Promised Land*. Other than fire ants and land crabs, I got it so good mostly, I will connect some more dots and finish up the missing connective tissue, by the time I close out another year *In the Life*.

It was in the early '80s when San Francisco became on every level too expensive to live in; sort of a double whammy on wage earners, both the big tax cuts and the propositions that led to property taxes being almost fixed or only rise by a very small percent. *Kaboom*. Landlords raise rents, that by now in 2023 are about 800+% higher than they were in '84 or so. Both my addictions and the fact that a few cops did have a genuine hard-on for me, I explore moving, offered a job in a Ferrari dealer in Portland, Oregon.

As I gather more info, I will add a page or two. Like Steve said, to begin in Florida and end there too.

WALKING MY BABY BACK HOME

I took a bus ride on the Grey Hound up there and walked from downtown all the way out to 122nd - I bet 15 or so miles. They were ready and glad to hire me. Went back, and by then I was living in a shell of a VW bus outside a junk yard; Nick Torelli's wife Nancy gave me $1000 and everything looked a bit more both stable and brighter.

An adventure of its own, Giatano Grambriloli lent me an Izuzu pickup truck. With my tools, it lasted from Frisco to Winters but I knew it would never make it and crap out long before Oregon. I stayed in Winters with Robert and Aline Crumb for a few days, got a U-Haul truck that I had to borrow money for, and Aline helped unload and load the tools in the U-Haul. One of Giatano's helpers came and got the small Pup truck and off I went.

I could really go on about the big changes in both my life and outlook after meeting the woman who is to this day my loving sister, and the men in Loyola AA group who both by example and a few rather harsh talks with me, got me off my own dumb ass, and 20 years of learning how to be a good man and not my own worst source of trouble. Married Murphy for 15 years, and another one to this day is my confidant and pal.

Things did change, to November of '05 when I came down to Florida. Again offered a job, 2 of them in fact, one to captain a fishing boat. That did not last a week; too drunk for me in the Keys. The other as the Roadside guy for Mercedes Benz; that paid as well as most all the other in the shop jobs I ever had. It left me lots of time off, but had this nasty habit of page me out at 2 am or so, most days 3 or 4 calls, at $50 a call to me, and my $100 a week for 3 months I was rolling on like Nolan. And o dear, got married *again*, but that ended rather quick; she is my friend now and we do not have to put up with eachother's odd traits.

Now, and of all days New Years Day 2023. Blast it all, lolly-gag and whimper or snarl, fuck all that running. Ever onward with good health and a better attitude and that bit of tropic splendor I call my back yard. What me worry? Only to fail myself again, by my life-long sort of under achieving and self-inflicted wounds. Nope! Not today. I had a quiet red cardinal come and it was to me all my old departed friends come to wish me well. Then a really noisy blue jay that was all the friends I have now wish me the same.

Intent and purpose…so changed because by then only stay out of trouble was good, as I learn a lot more about a life in recovery. The pages gone? Filled? Words expression contemplations ideas…changes daily to seem like it is all mixed up. Then the next page turns and I see where somehow all this makes a nice jello salad and got me some ginger ale on the side.

Have read so many things about writing; that whole thing about a lone voice and the nature of things. Seek it, speak it let the (bone clean) of it all. I do not really understand the motivation of it. I do have this chatter brain syndrome, sometimes, like 90 lines that do not say what 3 tight lines could. The process of telling some stories, recording some events, as a spectator one side, as a participant others.

I woke up from a terrible dream about drugs and prison, guns, and the prospect of getting killed, or worse, killing someone else over a bag full of alkaloid poison...them days are way behind me now. There is, I think, a lot about the cell memory of addictions and compulsions that always leads to defeat. What is a win? Being safe in your own skin; having that time space to enjoy the light changing the green of it, when it has a way of setting you to looking out at the same place but you see it differently. Like life, time and place, where the old stuff is memories, and the now stuff is get off your duff and do the work. Missing her, someone who's voice I have not heard in over 40 years now. That is not the kind of pain it used to be, because when you take a deep look at the results of your own failings, they are the lost days.

Dec 25, 2022. So far, told in pages my life in sort of bits and pieces, like I do everything ever, except auto repair, that most of my adult life was consumed by. On purpose leave out some guilt and shame, that to this day, *what's too painful to remember we just choose to forget*. On this of all days. It came upon a midnight clear, to the world was born a son. Used to be for a few hundred years, 25 December was the solstice. Julian came along and chopped off a few days. To how even now, I try to mark the days by the coming of the sun and fading of the day into night.

What is the meaning of setting down how many pages, to record, remember, and yeah, put up some adventures and some failures and to the time when my life became way more worth living? In the way I learn the things a lot of people learn way more earlier than I did about being honest and being accountable for thoughts words and deeds. I ponder some quote about how all words just disturb the silence. My hands are cold and I got on a big wool sweater; it is very cold here in Florida, today.

Back again…336 was the first time they made a big deal about Jesus being born and it was supposedly on January 6, that now is called Epiphany. I just happen to have one of those every few weeks, going over what does work and what is babble or snark. It took 4 of the last 7 years for me to both accept and even a bit enjoy living alone with limited social interactions, especially the last 3 years, where this pandemic had me really isolate. So funny, treating my own lonely with solitude and my angst with caffeinated black ground up beans.

Last year on this day, I went and spent some time with the dog who would become my roommate. I brought her home on January 14, and she's been one the best things ever to happen to me. I learn how to really care for (and be cared for) better with this four-footed wiggle ass mutt than I learned in 3 times married. That is the truth, in the current all day long you read about others and their history of abuse neglect and trauma. I am not laughing but, other than the time in that war in Vietnam, I can pretty much say all my abuse was self-inflicted. I do not do that anymore. I have been both blessed and gifted a place to live and a set of monthly bills and just able to keep myself afloat. How to end a memoir when the last pages have not happened yet? No way Jose, because the rest of my days are to be yet numbered or known. How the *GULP* end of it all happens. Nope, one more day even on Christmas, it all blends and mixes with the idea that what? the rest is yet the best is yet? I have no idea. Eat good, sleep good, don't lie cheat or steal, and man o man, I might just pull the rest of my life off with a bit o' style.

I had another very close friend, named Carlos Garcia, who lived up on Potrero Hill, and he was involved with a lot of jazz musicians and his house was a sort of meeting point. In this time frame, o how sweet it was, I was in love with a woman who lived on the other end of Gerke Alley. At Carlos' house was a lemon verbena bush; I would cut the flowering ends and put them under that woman's pillow. It was that scent and this perfume she would get from NYC called Paracelsus from Sara at the Knobkerry, a woman I knew well from my days in the Lower East Side in '66. Both of those smells and the linger of, are still in my cells. There was another woman on Fillmore St, a Japanese who owned a flower store, and I would trade her a lid of Panama Red for a magnificent arrangement that I too would leave in that woman's small apartment.

Why today, here in Florida in 2022, does all this flood into me? I am trying hard to have a bit of balance in the tale of all those years. This period of time was before cocaine and before big crime and my downfall. Last week, Florida experienced one of the most violent destructive hurricanes in a long time; Andrew and some others did not do this much damage. It led me on to going about cleaning up my yard now, and a spot where I am going to find and plant some lemon verbena, and yeah, the whole thing about Proust and memory of smells.

Wow, last few weeks, last few months, going over what why how and when I wanted to write this book. Then adding in, in my memory banks, the times in Frisco that were good, and then not ever get married again till 1989 in Oregon. Am I lonely? Is this book a memoir driven by both joy and sorrow? I think so, but to write, and live as well as I do now… one more time…if, as I have said, any dear reader who has themself struggled with addiction and self-punishment anger fear and doubt about being ever worthy of a good life: it happened to me and it can happen to you.

Going back over this one page, okay, I see myself on my bike put those lemon verbena stalks in my saddle bag and ride back to North Beach with a grin on my face wide as my face was. There is another part to this all too, the time in Oregon when I said I left because I did not want to be grandfather to someone else's kids; recall this when I was a good dad, and then when my whole life fell apart, all my own fault, in her teen-age years I was not there or even a bad dad for my Mary. I was at that point as useless to her as I was to myself. It took what it took, and when I look back and record it all…you never know; truly you never know.

I read to be inspired, I write to be released from my own nagging. The present and the future are all just an echo chamber of the past. I know that part, the what ifs, the yeah buts, all that maybe could a would a should a bullshit. I am about 11 years old; I already know I am being trained indoctrinated and sold this bill of goods. I am not able to tell anyone, other than my brother, Tommy, who already has made up his own mind about money is the answer. Reading then as much to escape as to be inspired. But, I read myths, I read stuff that no other 11 year old I know would. I vary my alter-self between Ed McBain and John D. McDonald. All that time living in an apartment with cracked walls and my by then pretty much late stage alcoholic mother. I know things, but I am helpless to escape in real time, the nagging I mentioned above. Why am I not one of those kids who got good houses and nice things? I bet if anyone reading all this can see that thread through and through, what I would later learn about self-esteem and never good enough issues that are a tribal similarity in just about every alcoholic I have met in my years of recovery. There is no way at that age I could have predicted the events to follow, a class structure that feeds a mass of those indoctrinated into the maw of death, in wars for profit. Yeah, at 14 I am already working for a living and have no idea about consequences tit for tat this and that. I don't.

It was 7 years ago today, I got those letters I had written to my junior high teacher, that would become the book *Dear Miss B*. This effort is to expand and fill in the years after those letters. I am still amazed that I was found and sent those letters. I read my 18-year-old, 19-year-old self, and hear that 11-year-old talking to himself about there must be a better way. I would so many years later know fully the only better way is the one you make. If allowed to, that nag scold complain will drag you to that hollow place where you give up on it all. I will not, not now, not ever. The next month or so maybe more time even, I am going to find the echo chamber and silence some of that, into new voice new ideals and caring. I've been so blessed with the help I get, and now the proof in all that is how I do this, *page by page…*

THEY ASKED ME HOW I KNEW

I have looked back now at so many of the changes…I must jump to getting put in prison where, for the first time since Vietnam, I really did question who causes you to be fucked with, and how much of it is your own dumb doing or bad luck. **BAD LUCK AND TROUBLE** was a really cool patch I had sewn on one of my saddle bags, the one on the other side said **EAT BUGS BE HEALTHY**. Between the forks, hanging from the goose neck, was a Tibetan prayer bell, and on the back light it said **SAFETY FIRST**. I got to think over some things while I was feeling like a bucket of hammered who cares? One of them was, it occurred to me, about getting wised up after they close that East Gate on me in Folsom; like when before I got to Vietnam, it was some great adventure, you know freedom's frontier, kill a commie for mommy and make the world safe for good biddness (or some shit).

To the first day in prison and knowing it ain't about luck at all, it is about *choices*. "Who's ya daddy?" Some people got a pass at ever having to be responsible, they just ease by it all. Me? Responsible meant you had to play by the rules. The week I knew I was really gonna get out of prison, my, "Fuck you I won't an you can't make me," was flushed down the toilet of time. It became "I don't know how," but I was damned if I was not going to find some people to show me how.

Choices. If you don't have your bike in good shape and know the limit of adhesion, you are very likely to take a nosedive over the handlebars and wind up roadkill. Same with way more mundane things - pay attention, be your own road guard before you wind up getting carried by six to the end of anything. I never even thought about getting killed in the war in the crimes on the crazy road running. But now, I do think about being dead, and I ain't got no real eyes for that at all. Ever onward, till either the canvas come up to kiss you or the night demon has its claws in your neck; that last boat ride, up into the mystic, is not one I want to get a ticket to any time soon.

All I need is the air that I breathe, an you. Yeah, couple of days here of late that first part came pretty hard. No energy, and very short of that air. Funny, how when you're in the middle of something and you don't have the juice or go power to work on it. Ideas, thoughts, a cavalcade of memories, and what did happen, what has been and has not been already written. Did I confuse a few years here or a couple of days there?

Going over it, myself, I figure out this other stance: I am not all that important dead at all, with a back side thinking about not being all that important alive either. I've been told and read that writing is mostly a solitary endeavor. I see it more as reaching out, calling on, calling to. The pages, the stages, the going and coming, in and out of both time place, and where do you find a deeper connection with words and ideas. I got some other really good advice about not using the books I am reading to go off on some idyllic direction, with either history or fantasy. Yeah, and then I saw about your own distractions are only mental burps, and duck weave feint for not seeing yourself as very important. Old Hemingway said it is okay to steal stuff long as you make it better. I have my own take on that: Sometimes just read a line and sit there astounded, at both the similar and the different way people see the same thing and see it 9 ways from Sunday. I do that sometimes; I know I do.

Everything you've been taught or told was all lies, or mere agenda of the power mad and those who use anybody and everybody they can. And had there been the internet then, some of the stuff I write here and have posted on my Facebook page, shit, they would have confiscated my computer and give me life without. Why's this now hit me so hard? Well, I read about three books a week, every week, sometimes five. If they are potboilers I even skip over pages when they say who said what to who and why. I can usually tell who done it pretty much less than halfway in. Then a more serious tome, I take my time and digest it. I can clear remember reading the Ed Snowden book, and thinking the net has made trade craft and dead drops and all that trench coat spy bullshit obsolete. Data mines? Yeah, the low rent suck butts are just trying to scam you or beat you out of some money. The more danger is in the cops and the DEA the NSA FBI all of them, who got bots and real people just scan you troll you or look where you been and who and what you researched.

Yeah, okay. I am bound here to tell the truth, I am, both funny, sad, good and bad. My own life? These years alive, born in the fall out of the atom bomb, and I bet you I got some DNA stuff that would make the nuns blush if they knew. In my last book I laid out the war I had with the Catholic Church, at 11 or 12 years old. Coming up will be (next book) my 20 years as Orthodox and find out even more lies about the real nature of both religion and salvation, to how the ones who preach the most about the deadly sins do them, just about all of them, all of the time. Now, what has me set off this evening, I am reading this book called *Echos of Eden*, and the guy lays out all that stuff I have ranted and raved about for years. If God so loves you and all of us, why do we just kill each other all the time and use the worst kind of propaganda to insulate and hide the really guilty. Not like mafia hit guys who wack maybe 10 people for money, I mean the ones who kill millions to get their portfolio fatter.

O well, never mind all of that.

I am on the corner of 19th and Mermaid Ave in 1959, and I meet Loretta DeGagnero, who I find out is crazy about my cousin who then was a minor criminal in the making; who would become indeed a big mob boss. She was in my 4th and 5th grade class. We talk a bit about all that and, I later find out, she and him are already playing more than kiss and fondle. Yup, but what is the makeup of who you knew and when you knew them?

To this day where I know the people who like or love me as I do them, it's not about romance. Sometimes about finance, I got to admit. This whole effort unwinding before me... I had some really great days, I really did. On Elsie St and in North Beach, I labor too much here about the fall and not enough about the good stuff.

Ana Heartman from the hot dog stand, a full-blown Trotsky believer, and she got her car towed I went and got it with her and fix it up just so, and, yeah, good times. When I introduce her to Spain and the 2 of them go on for hours about Stalin and Trotsky, she never ever backed down nor did he. She helped me a lot when I got hurt on a bike, and nursed me good. She moved to Boston, I think, but that year when she and I were lovers or like that, comfort. And I never did understand the stuff she talked about, other than when I took her for motorcycle rides, and we ate good.

Some of them are so far gone now I can *only* remember them, fondly, and with that mix of when it did go bad, had I just listened to the ones who warned me, and tried to comfort me when I could not comfort myself in just about any way... To now, my reading, my writing and my bust out attempt to make some order out of all this jumble of what was, what happened, what is now.

About time to try and wrap this up with a bow. Besides the flip around chronology and ending now in a very well cared for safe space, I ponder and wonder all at the same time about going from counting stacks of money from either dope deals or safe jobs, to now I put all my coin change in a cup so if it is tight I can use that money as backup when my month to month falls short. Going on 17 years in Florida, where I came to be a fish bum at 60 and just give up on everyday wrestle with automobiles. As it would turn out, my first week in the Florida Keys was not at all what I thought it would be. They're very drunk down there, and call it the

Conch Republic, a host of scalawags and imported out from up north or places even more distant. Then my phone call from New Jersey at Mercedes corporate headquarters, and an offer I could not refuse. Roadside guy all over the Treasure Coast and inland almost to this side of Lake Okeechobee. I did that for 5 years, on and off only get paged when there was a call out. I did do a few side jobs, but never take jobs away from the shop, and there were a few that I had towed and the foreman asked me to fix them. My call outs were $50 to me, and if I did any work on any of them it was at 30-some an hour. I never had to replace a motor or transmission, only electric or hydraulic repairs, at book time.

That fish bum part? O yeah, with the boat I had towed behind my pickup truck, that I still have with 300k miles on. I would go all over the St Lucie and Indian Rivers, up back cross both sides. On a good day I could get snook, jacks, lady fish, some pompano, sea trout, and I only ever kept what I was gonna eat. I had some friends who had offshore boats and would go out deep and get mahi grouper snapper and made feasts out of them. On one rainy night at just over 65 years old, I was at 2am on the turnpike changing a flat tire. I had told the guy at the local tackle shop, Snook Nook, I was really tired of working and the in and out at all hours. He told me, "Go upstairs and fix fishing reels, the guy there now got his own shop and I think he is a bit sloppy on my reels."

I had taken care of my own stuff for years, so what the hell. About a week after that 2am call, I bagged that roadside job. I did for 9 years work most days when there were reels to fix and made about 60% or so of my Mercedes pay, but it was way more easy and way more fun. Especially getting to know most all the charter guys and big-time offshore captains.

They often would tip me with some caught that day filets. I left one time, a bit bored and wanted to really work on my writing, but the guy who they got was not at all capable, so they asked me to come back and I did. In 2016, the election and the, what I see as, the time of, "My guy my way this way the only way." I did get in a pretty heated argument with 2 of the guys there and knew in my bones it was time to go and stay gone.

It was not until March of this year I went back and just stop in and make amends to one and the other one had moved on. I do not need anything in the tackle shop now, and fishing in the river is not all that good at all now due to the political admins of the last 10 years who have allowed the sugar and agriculture industries to use the big lake as their toilet, and then that foul water is discharged into the rivers.

End with a bow? Ha, one of the things I am sure of now is there're more days gone than days left. I have to sell off or give away a bunch of stuff, so my daughter does not have to clean up all my junk. Excuse me, all my treasured possessions; again ha. I am pretty sure I've already written the way I got this house and the fact I've been here now since late 2014 and make it all the time more mine and more both visual- and hygiene-wise the best it can be. I've been for the last few months planting roses, cabbage palms, flowering bushes, and making the yard look like I am trying to get into *Home and Garden* magazine. That's all part of living now, even as I write about some of the bad days and who and what I was then, the closing pages make it clear, it is about changes. How I came, first stumble, then run head long out of the dark into the light.

I almost want to add some pages about my dog, Murphy Quinn, or, my nick name for her, The Black Streak. She can run so fast her four feet are like a cartoon, go 'round and kick up dust. I think or feel the rest of my story that I do know has some time left to live and tell. There will be an end spot, to call out with love and gratitude for the few years now I have said I am doing this book, and some of them sent me an email or a message about when they were there and saw a few things I did not. How you fill up any book story or poem is about feelings and knowings and thinking it all over. I remember some things with absolute clarity, some I know deep in my heart...I chose to not want to say or even have that burden of guilt or shame on my plate.

In the year or so it has taken me to put this down page by page, the world has changed a lot. Just to say not all that much for the better. Even if some of us, I hope many of us, have found a way to deal with both the political foolery and the virus and the wide losses of ones loved. In thinking I am really about 5 years into this book, and I do not know what to really call it other than a memoir or a listing of, one more time, out of addictions and sorrow into just about as peaceful and content as I have ever felt. That said, my heart does bleed for the shared sorrow of so many. If by some way hope dream, putting all this down and one person sees it reads it and makes it to the *moment of clarity*, that is how the trail time real time in recovery begins.

I could have, I bet you, spent a lot of pages here going back to where it seems to start in 1946 to now 2023, and list from the atom bomb to Vietnam to JFK to RFK, Martin Malcolm Fred Hampton Mark Clark, the FBI the DEA, the CIA, all of it, an learning myself how we are only as sick as our secrets. On the pages I have cried bled and work about one half the other and all in between. There can never I think be a perfect ending beginning or middle, just doing what Alexander Pope said in the 1600s. Each and every day I try to be better in each and every way. The tasks of now take me out of then, with what I like to think is put it down and let it go. Into not lost afraid depressed or wishing some of it had not happened; that too.

    I also must admit, in spite of sounding like some bad ass biker thug and bum, I have always had a very soft side, and am as I been told sometimes very sappy. Because I do allow a range of feeling and emotions to roam around as they will. Through the last 5 years there are about 15 people who have encouraged me, helped me and add to my intent and purpose of doing another book. Baby, the rain must fall, I am not rich or famous and I really don't want to be. The years up in Oregon, when I was a radio personality, gave me all the fame I ever want. Even if it did lead to 3 trips back to Vietnam and a video of 2 other guys and me who went to DC and visited the memorial wall. *Memories at the Wall*, I hear it is on YouTube now. I am not who or what I was all that time ago, and not all that sure of what I am now, but way more sure of who I am.

ALL THE PLACES AND THINGS

Far back, when my dad would come home from work at about 7am...He would make breakfast and pack bag lunches for me and my brother. Then he would lie in bed and cover his face with his hand and pray himself to sleep. Way later, 60 years or so, my brother Tommy would become very devout; as a lifelong gambler, I wonder if he was just hedging his bets. On his last day in hospice, I was holding his hand, his feet were moving under the sheet, he opened his eyes an said clear, "I am going home," and died.

With me the only one to still be alive of my 5 person birth family. I have been asked why I do not write or talk about my other brother Bobby. His life was, I think in a lot of ways, way more difficult than mine. I also think he was born with fetal alcohol syndrome. Sometimes that old thinking stuff makes me understand and be way more forgiving than for the so many years I was not. I am going to add that forgiving myself was the doorway to open into a mostly forgiving attitude. I have to this day, and I refuse to call them resentments or regrets about, some things objects machines that I miss as much as I miss any person. The whole daily deal now is about, upon awaking, to make that vow over about, just for today, there will be no booze dope or God help me no lies crime or theft. That alone, with the proviso that my only choices now are based on some 30 years of doing things, if not better, at least not worse. Yeah, the most part of this book is 30 some years ago and 30 some pounds ago. At 163 now, from between 185 and 195 most my adult life. Did breaking my neck change my metabolism? I don't know. Does having way less stress and angst about whatever it was I had done and when would it catch up with me help? I bet my best fishing rod, it sure does.

It was a long way from Coney Island to Vietnam, and back again to San Francisco, Oregon, and now in Florida. I live here for, I think, the rest of my days; I do not see another move. Given the economic time and prices, I bet I could never live this well anywhere else. A song of life or *a song of love is a sad song* (some time) *Hi, Lili, hi, Lili, hi lo*. Other than when I get some either editorial commentary or instructed to alter change or add to, I think I about put this baby to bed. I have 3 more poetry collections in process. I want to publish them and leave a bit of me in ink, as it seems my days now got less of them left than the ones been already gone.

Caught up in a tale of so many failures, mixed with a lot of years of redirection, and relieved of pitiful incomprehensible demoralization. A balance point, of learning to live within my means, allowing needs to be way more important than wants. A line from Herman Hesse, "The frequent access to melancholy and despair is linked to the knowledge all desire is but a fleet and transitory experience." That and, my own now rolling along page by page, try to get the balance point of wasted time to productive and, I think I already said, at least content. That too, as how many years now subject to my moods, where I can have a good day and turn it into a sadness with some old failures come to mind. In anything about life, time place and people, humor is needed to adjust the flame. I once heard a 90-year-old priest say he would rather burn out than rust out. I think that sometimes. Anyone who has read this far along, sees as I do the burn out could have happened many times. How can I not throw in these days you could get shot at the supermarket by a random bullet?

That makes me remember in training group one time, this hard ass NCO, back from Vietnam, says there is a Viet Cong has a bullet with your name on it. My buddy Madison laughs, and the guy gets all red in the face, "You think that is funny?"

Madison, as he did all the time, "I ain't sure any of em know my name but a bullet addressed to whom it may concern does worry me." The whole room just cracked up, even the NCO gave a tiny smile. There were some really serious training briefs, and at that time the war was not even a big deal, but it sure became one.

I have had so many chances to change, and until I really did, there were some times, now I recall that I did know better, I just did not care enough about myself to make the effort. It does take serious work to undo years of what is called stinking thinking, and self-will run riot. Even now, when I go back and forth about the nature of God, or the idea that there is so much beyond our knowing, no matter the route step mumble prayers and hope for salvation. I take that both ways what a great story it is that parts of gospel, that tell you you're saved if you do this that or the other. When to me it is still a great mystery of how I learned how to accept a power greater than myself, that was in my case both words and by example of others who had lifted themselves out of desperation into productive and good lives. There were a few men and women who explained to me about, "Let go, or be dragged." I worry about repeating myself or using the same phrases over, but once I found out that only staying out of trouble or jail was only a small part of overall recovery…mentioned as I have, the first cocaine episodes where it seemed like clarity of thought, it was delusion. To the real clarity of both thoughts and actions, that did not have punishment attached to them. Self-punish or legal ones.

It has been suggested to me to fill in some more of good times, good jobs, like the one on the radio for 4 years. Some more garage tales and bit more early things in Coney Island and Neptune's Arms. Mr. Emerson, "Nothing great was ever achieved without enthusiasm." Well far from me to call this great, it needs to be both lyrical and entertaining as I can make it. I have a very close friend named Judith Jones, who is a many-year therapist, and she has both advised me and counselled me on what I can only call better direction. I do take knowledge from others who, for however long, know me, or have some insights I do not. How many more pages left to go? As many as it takes to feel like the result was worth the effort.

It is about mid-year of 1996. I am working for Town and Country dealerships as a used car mechanic. One day Ralph Martinez, the big boss, comes into my stall with a paper in his hand. Tells me, "Dom, you got to go over to KXL radio over in West Lynn an get this job."

I look over at him and tell him I got to put this car back together. He just laughs and tells me, "It is a used car, it can sit there a week. Go do what I told you."

So, knowing he knows more than I do about all things business but have no idea what a radio station would want out of me. I go out and get my truck, Stinky, an '85 S-10 pick-up with a killer motor and smells like old cigars. I look at the paper...it is a notice for a mechanic to become the Hi-way Helper. I got no idea but am intrigued. Not all that fancy a building, but the reception desk is very clean and an older woman is behind it. She takes the paper and tells me, "Yes, there was a phone call saying you were on the way. Have a seat an I will tell them you are here."

She tells me a couple of minutes later, go upstairs and Loretta will show you where to go. I do, and I am shown into the sales-manager office. Tim McNamara, the station manager, and the sales guy and program director are all sitting there. Tim greets me and says, "Mr. Martinez told us you are a perfect fit for what we are looking for." I sit down and am not nervous or any more than very curious what this could be all about.

Mike Evans, the program director, starts in with, "We want to put a Hi-way Helper on the roads during rush hours and aid stranded motorists and call in reports during our normal traffic ones. The ODOT has already told us they would be glad for the help and would be willing to train for a week someone who they approve of to do that job." The sales guy, who for the life of me I cannot remember his name, says, "We have a couple of sponsors lined up and this will be a full-time job with very good pay."

I am at a loss of what to say. But, given my glib and what's been called an outsize personality, I say, "I do know a bit about the radio an TV business an cannot for the life of me think why this sort of altruistic help is gonna both pay an work out."

Tim gets up, says, "This is the guy; get the paperwork started an put him on."

I spend about an hour filling out a booklet and they want to know what grammar school I went to and what auto repair certificates I have, and the last line is: after a drug test, we will notify you of your next step. I start to laugh, and the lady looks over at me like what do you think is funny, and I tell her drug tests are ones I do not have to study for. She laughs, and I get sent to this piss test place pee in the cup and go back to work. I do not hear anything for a couple of days and figure it was a bust.

Ralph comes in my stall, "You got the job, I am going to provide the vehicle, go over to the Chevy store see my brother Robert an get a new Suburban, then have somebody follow you to the decal an paint place."

I am stunned and do not even know what to say or do. I tell Ralph I love my job here and really this the longest time I ever worked in one place if it goes bust can I come back here. He looks a bit miffed, "I have told you a number of times, all you have done for me an now I want to do this for you, it will not go bust, an they are gonna pay you twice or more what you make here." I could've died right then and there. I go get the Suburban and take it down to the painting place. I have my buddy take me back to the shop where for about 2 hours I finish this one used car then send it to detail and go home.

I had told Mary Catherine, my wife, a bit about this job deal, but now I told her I got the job, and next week I go ride with COMET, the ODOT guys, and learn how to be a roadside helper and what they say I can and cannot do. She, as I recall, is of mixed feeling because the time, about 9 or so years, with Town and Country has been very stable and really good pay. She asks me if I really want to do this and I tell her I am a born ham and getting to talk on the radio's been a big dream of mine for years. She and I go in front of the icons and we both pray about God's will and our life.

O man, 2 weeks riding around with 3 different state workers; one of them was really sour on the whole idea but did warm up a bit when I told him I ain't about to try and be a hero out here, I got all the trouble I want in my life years ago. We come up on a wreck, 3 cars; we both get out, have cones to mark off the lane, and one woman looks like she may be hurt. I open her door, and Ed, the state guy, pulls me back, "Never touch any one ever. Do not get yr self in some lawyer's happy feet to sue you." The cops, the ambulance show up, and 2 tow trucks. The guy tells me that dealing with wrecks, you will find out, is the worst part of all this. I do not know the conversation with the radio station and the ODOT, but it is clear from the program director who I go see, "They gave you a really good review and go get the vehicle you start next week."

Loretta, the lady who it seems does all the admin and like that, hands me a cell phone and another one. "This one is for you, and you can use it like it is your own; the second one is only for radio use an it is how you will call in your reports." I have that phone number to this day. I have had to replace the phone but stuck to a flip phone that still has my number now. I go get the Hi-Way Helper vehicle. I am about to fall over. They have put an orange flashing light bar on the roof, and big **KXL 750** and **CHEVRON** decals, and on both doors in cursive letters it says *DOMINIC*, you could've slapped me and not make me more excited.

    I got to meet all the news crew, and the producers, like Shawn Taylor and Carolyn Myers; Steve and Rebecca were the news anchors in the AM and PM with talk shows Lars Larson and Michael Savage, and Dave and Dwight comedy hour in between, There was attached an FM station, JAM-MING 95, owned by Rasheed Wallace of the Portland Trail Blazers. The AM part was owned by Paul Allen, co-founder of Microsoft. I got to learn how to email and got my own email address at the station and was shown how the phone call recording process went. An editor named Mike would get my calls and clean up any static or road noise. It would be a week of going back and forth to the station and to all the local Chevron stations to introduce myself. The other sponsor then was State Farm Insurance. I would later find out the ad bills were in the 300K range.

    They offered me 90K for a year or so, then would review both the program and any further sponsorship ads. I can remember fully clear just driving on the different freeways and feeder roads and was told by the next week to stop and help anyone stranded on any of those roads. It was a Monday morning, the news hour was 5am to 10 am and 3pm to 6pm, with feeds from CBS national news on the hour, traffic reports on the 8-minute mark.

After traffic, they would play my reports. "Up on 205 near Glisan St, a lady with a flat tire in a VW. I change to her spare an she had Krispy Kreme donuts. This is Dominic the KXL Chevron Hi-way Helper."

Rebecca says, "He can smell donuts all the way to Vancouver."

It went on like that for a few weeks as I got my feet wet, and really felt like I got this. I did. They would get calls saying how much they like the hi-way helper, and some people even wanted a photo to see what I looked like, so they put up a billboard with the truck and me waving out the window. **KXL'S OWN HI-WAY HELPER.** Some of the reports were really funny, "On 5 south and there are 2 cars pulled over with one guy waving an empty gas can. Well kids, you know I got 20 gallons in my rig. Gas em both up an off they went."

The boss loved that one, and explained to me the real trick is, "Be brilliant be brief and be gone." I never forgot that, and Mike, my voice editor, sometimes would tell me, "Do it again shorter an do not get all preachy on me or we gonna have a problem." Some days while I was off the road Dave and Dwight would call me to jabber about the road, and one time, "What would you do if you had to deliver a baby?" Snort and giggle, "I got a lot o WD 40 on board."

I bet I could go on for a few more pages about those years. It was the highest paid job I ever had and took my Social Security payment from about 900 to 1600 a month. I would sometimes visit the JAMM 95 hip-hop studio and jive with E Bro, and some of those ribald comments I made did not sit well at all with Mr. McNamara. I did not go over there again, other than one time to fix a car for one of the female DJs but did not say a word on or off the air about dumb shit that has followed me all these years. Beside the pay, it was also easy, even the hardest parts like wrecks or cars that were way beyond any roadside help. I did have really good tow truck contacts.

The paycheck went into a joint account with me and Mary Catherine. She would give 5 or 10 bucks a day for my fruit pie and chocolate milk. There were some public speaking events too, the state fair and some local Chevron stations. At one, a fund raiser for a girl name Deena with brain cancer raised over 50thousnd bucks. I was the grand marshal at the Sandy Mountain Days parade. I still have that T-shirt. Again, the time went by, I would visit Town and Country and Herzog Myer and one other garage I worked at, and they all would tell I found my place.

Butch, a VW mechanic who was wounded really bad in Vietnam - the bottom his jaw gone, he used to wear a T shirt that said *Don't Ask Me I Was Hired For My Looks* - he and I were very close, and it was him who told me almost a year before 9/11 there was gonna be more war. On 9/11, I got taken off the road, and by about a week later, both State Farm and Chevron had pulled out the paid sponsorship. Ralph called all the dealerships to a meeting, and I spoke about the trouble and need for us to unite. The other part was, since it had been like 24 hour a day news, the whole staff was exhausted working double shifts, I did come in and run some supply runs, and tried to be helpful. The program director, Mike, had moved over to the competitor station 1190 owned by Clear Channel. The new guy, James, was way younger and way more about how they were going to re-structure the whole station. Lars was in his top form, a sort of imitation Rush Limbaugh, and that was very tiresome to me. Tim the manager of it all, said, "We are going to eliminate a lot of things. You get 3 months' pay, an bring the vehicle back to Mr. Martinez."

I got my old job back, but got offered an even more attractive one at Major Murrey in Milwaukee working on classic cars, and Ralph was in the process of selling off about 5 or 6 stores, and consolidate his operation to 3. No hard feelings at all.

I went to work at Major and got to play with old American cars, some of them real classics and some of them worn out old piles of junk. I drove by the BMW shop around the corner, and went in. The guy there, Mark Dekos, knew me and said he would offer me a full time good job to work on early BMWs. I did that for 3 years, even had my old pal Gerry from Ferrari come help me convert a 30csi to a 533i. Took weeks. Some guy in that shop had tried and he just messed it up so bad and came up with every bullshit excuse you could imagine. Mark fired him and Gerry and I got it, not only running but, running well.

My then stepdaughter, Adrienne, at 17 with the next door boy, came home with a baby. 2 years later another baby. Boys Justice and Cassian, the younger one was a real trial. Seemed like I was the one who could calm him. I would walk him and sing to him. It wore me down, and it would lead to my big decision to leave for good and move to Florida. I have a wonderful plaque the Church gave me for 20 years of service, and the priest had mixed feelings but did bless us to work it out. We divorced and those pay checks? I had way more money than I knew and Mary Catherine was very fair with me, gave me almost 20thousand dollars, a long jump from the 1800 or so I had left Frisco with 20 years ago.

Hop, skip, jump back 20 years and leaving Frisco. When the Ferrari dealer closed, I was over in Oakland a lot helping Alfredo, and not making much money, but, like he would say, we don't make much money but we have lots of fun. He was very close friends with a couple of Jaguar mechanics and the service manager at British Motors of SF. He sent me over there and I got a job as the only Maserati mechanic. O boy, I did have some times with those cars, the Bora most of all. One time got chased by the cops and outran them. Neckties on the ramp with badges, and on my squawk box, "Fekking what have you done now?"

I answer him, "Why me?"

He said, "It is always you," and Jock the dispatcher saved my ass. He told them no Maserati left the shop today. Cost me 2 lids of Panama Red. In another speeding and, I admit, driving like an idiot, incident, the owner of that car saw me on 280 and I bet I was in triple digit speed Bill Miles, the service manager, let me go.

I went over to Marin County and worked for about a year at Mellow Motors. What a shop that was, VW, Alpha, and 3 of my old Ferrari owners brought their cars there for me to service. Drugs, one more time…Rick, who I am in contact with now, said it be better if I leave. And I did. I went to work at Mill Valley BMW as the used car guy. What a time that was, neat cars, and a sales manager more addicted to coke than I was. A few of the mechanics were, too. I got a BMW Bavaria that Nancy and I would drive in 7 western states for a month. Visit my old pals in Tucson, too.

I just cannot labor over that part, because after that trip she went to Asia for a year, and it was the year of my undoing. I have already told of our parting, and my later state paid up state vacation behind walls at Folsom.

GONE TO REST

I really at this point, do not know what other parts to include or leave out. I do want to wrap it up with a bow on, like I said, lighter more funny more positive living, like I live now. There are only 2 things I am about deathly afraid of: Gypsies and Horses. So this cannot be some wagon pony story. I did last year get a dog. I think the tales of Murphy and me would make a better kids' book than to go on here about all our adventures and the times now with her that have chased all the lonely out of this house. I bet at some point in every writer's work, they wait for some editorial commentary and feedback from who they trust and who knows their work. The offer to write and publish this book was to me a giant step up from my many poetry books, where indeed I did get feedback - and Donna Lee, Kris Haggblom, and Judith did a lot of that - about them before publishing them The reviews after are like my awards, really, some pretty well known writers have said the books are real tight and very good to read. My Vietnam poem book was used in

3 coll.ege classes about that war. I have been invited and showed up at 2 of them to give an hour-long talk on writing and my process of time, place, people, and things. I once gave a whole reading only about motorcycles, bicycles, and cars. I have 2 more collections on cars, that for some reason never really got me to like them enough to get them in a book.

BUT I'M LEAVING ONCE AGAIN

WHEN

each entrance or
exit
to the fun house
is barred
not just closed for the season
but entombed by
mold weeds....detritus
memories of slaked thirst
go-kart quick chemical relief
sparkle lines of Bolivian
bitter lines of what now is
not in the cards
either dealt or on a shelf
marked

forbidden fruit
one is left to ponder
idly curious ...or enmeshed
reality....shift .....tide change....shore line
width......mental seascape ...of long ago
when....a mood a feeling a circumstance
could be altered ...obliterated.

...dusted disgusted not
to be trusted
or shake n shimmy.....coming down
only age can give you
with a smirk...of *been there done that,
got the yellow sheet n t-shirt*
afternoon contemplatives... polishing rocks...
gems....semi-precious stones
of
things now....distant
but
only a jar or 8 ball away
nope
not today
I own my mind do not rent it or give it away
for
pleasure or pain
sober n dare I say...
almost content content about now

Life goes on and on even when it seems like an old sad song it's not something you get over but it's something you get thru "Willy Nelson" Last Man Standing... as this in this time line when for 6 years now running since *Dear Miss B*...and my new one every poem I have ever written is a part of how *It's Not Something You Get Over*...into as this new book is wrapping up there is gonna be some happy feet and a few real giggles cause the other line about "when you lose the one you love" as for this very day....I know deep in my bones I got all the time left I do to be a bit better in each and every way...cause the dumb shit and drugs guns and money...are *exactly* what I said about hand cuffs

FOR ONE THING

I don't wanna believe
it is luck
or high born order
class race location family or friends
(even when you grow yr own family outta dust)
nope
some flame out some rust
giant ideas an (propositions) go
bust
ya can go buy all the tools in a Snap On
truck
if ya don't know how to use em
yr fucked
circumstances or again (luck)
what ends in the ends of it
think some if I get the answer
I will
give ya
a call
  .

ALTERING APPEARANCES

either sartorial or emotional
with
thrift store abandon or in
barber chairs or....scribble in...notebooks
illuminate ruminate or expose
all of the nasty...all of the hall of mirrors
each person...in daily choice to be
loving one's self...loathing one's self
between crumpet...or tea hours ..or solitary confinement
sitting just anywhere...in a bag of skin....clipped some
strange way to bones....veins .....photographs
being more touch stone ......dim....or vibrant
illustrated or out of focus........time place between stops
for
however long
a place a bit of....safe space
recording...trying to remember....what is real
what is hoped for....not....dreams or wishes
but
that part of words...that the pages only prove
somebody once said, something
meaningful then IT CAN BE DONE
write away anger
write away fear
walk away, clear
Now it has been done
a dozen different ways
the "War Movie"
bullshit

When you are 18
years old
and watch your
best "got your six"
buddy
pockmarked full of bullets
GONE FOREVER you cry
you do not die
yet the survivor
sometimes has pain
the flag draped coffin never did will not ever
fill the empty space
O yeah they wrote
books about it
they gave talks about
it
The VA is like
Mr Rogers neighborhood.
even the "outreach"
staffed by guys who do know
staffed orders that
are paper bound to
"provide service and benefit"
well again reading, talking
no one understands
when the boots
are full of blood
the eyes close
game ends
in grave holes ground
if you been there

it takes longer
than forever
to come back
the writing the singing
 make up
do break up
that knot that ball
of anger
fear
why did they die
who made the profit
what price is worth a frame box
of medals and a triangle folded flag
as some hot shot
plays golf
reads his "investment status"
well you can only wonder
cause there is no fair
only word by word
replaces the doubt
it will all
work out

ALL THINGS MUST END

Working, thinking, writing, have that angst where if you could you would chew off ya own feet.

Adding a few of my poems, without asking for any more myself to be able to finish this with by tie up some out of order time frames. Asking myself about what needs to be in that is not and what just should be left out.

In just about 10 or so years now that creating a new family out of dust... Not quite, it takes this effort of connection direction similar interests and needs. In order to understand either online or in person interaction, that part about our own both failings and victories in what we all either survive or succumb to. Some days, I swear my own inner dialog is full of obituaries. Lingering over some memory and the phone rings. It is a today person, with, "Hey, we going to see this movie do you wanna come with us?" Liberation from mulling over what is gone. Or it is a long-distance call, just checking in, simple as how is the weather, or a terrible even like someone just died.

A big jump forward for a change. Knowing full well now the depth and width of my own deceptive ways, and selfish self-centered, without consideration for needs or wants of others. I took a lot of time to sort out the parts of my life.

Hey, it's Friday night, the mechanics' night out. She laughs and says, "Sounds like a Hungarian movie."

I just stare at her. Ask her what it's gonna take to get anywhere with you, the look, o man that look. Do you really wanna know? I take a sip of coffee and say I would not ask you if I did not. OK, you are funny you're very quick and, it seems to me, you have got a few wires crossed in your ideas about women. O, at this point, I can feel it coming, and we get up and go for a walk up Columbus to Washington Square Park, nice time of day, colorful sky, and evening just starts to fall. We sit on the bench outside Flor De Italia, and we had been flirting and have coffee and even once gone to Speck's had 2 beers and a plate of string cheese. I have not been in a relationship now for a year and you need to hear me tell you this, and do not start in on the why buts or and OK? Yup, I am very attracted to you, and know a bit about your disaster with him; I never liked that guy anyway. Well, you do not get any points for that, nobody seems to like him much anyway. As for you and I, first off, this is not an insult, but your pants always smell like gasoline, and that motorcycle you ride looks like some b grade ou-law biker movie, and I have seen you at Gino and Carlo with a few guys I know to be out and out criminals. Now I am really interested, and my first crack is I will change that Lake injector on my bike that is where the gas sprays on my pants when I nail the throttle. But there was more, she then says, your beard is a different color than your hair; for some reason that makes me very leery about get further involved with you. Hmm, I did have a dark red beard then and sort of very light hair from being on the beach surfing. OK, and then, I think to myself, without saying much more, I am going to win her, or think I am. We get up, and I take her hand, let me sort out some things, and let this Friday go, and I ask you now, for next Friday, and dinner and a movie, OK? She looked at me with a pair of the most tender eyes on earth, Yes, pick me up but not on the bike, OK? I left, and sufficient to say, I showed up in a Maroon Ferrari 330 clean shaven, with flowers and a smile. We were lovers for over a year, when she moved to NYC. We left each other on a long walk to Ft Point, and under the GG bridge she kissed me and told me she would not be afraid of men anymore, and this was a wonderful part of my life; we spoke on the phone a few times as she settled in. A few months later she called me and was giddy happy and told me she met someone and knew she was going to marry him. They came to Frisco for their honeymoon, and, when she introduced me to him, she said this is one of my closest ever friends and you might want to thank him; he showed me how to love again…1974 know what…we love each other still…I get a phone call every year or so. And they are still married and doing well.

If I were a traded stock, I sold myself short every time. I bet I could have been a really good actor. I can memorize stuff really easy and have this what someone once called an outsize personality. I did get to pretty much the top of the car repair trade. Those years on the radio were like acting, too. Anyone who thinks or says they got where they are alone and did it all themselves, is either an ego maniac or a fool. My case my times it is clear, without even a doubt, it was other people who both taught me and nurtured me along. When I would have this holding on to old ideas or schemes, my AA sponsor would say, "How well did that work out for you?" I now have a list of many names, and see their faces, hear their voices, who have supported me in a lot ways and been there for me in times I was, if not lost, for sure not knowing where I was or heading to.

Ferlinghetti..."the drunk nay bobs on Nob Hill who did not like it called Frisco" (I riff off this myself)....being just about cripple drunk but stable enough to kick start my chopper roar down Filbert to Columbus peel ass onto Broadway thru the defiant acceleration blast out the tunnel weave a bit onto Van Ness, part sober now wind clear mind boggled anyhow all the way to Market all most dump it turn into Valencia headed for Mission and Army pull up front of El Zocalo to get pupusa and some relief from acid rum sit still eat the cheese n salad and not get beer only water now no longer sideways walking run goose it to Virginia left on Winfield right on Esmeralda back home to 101 Elsie.................never ask where I been why ask when I might just lie anyhow shatter scatter sorrow over the wife n kid gone to 20th Street tired of my madness and criminal sidekicks all fall down on the now single bed where just 2 years ago my baby's crib was take it all in let it all out some 47 year ago hungover morning the next day and as if it comes out my darkest yet to be place clear recall ask myself how bad can this all really get...*101 ELSIE STREET* few more months...this is an experiment in free flow dangle words like old hippy love beads...at the age I would a been a beatnik I was otherwise occupied in Asia

EXISTING

no living
breathing
blooming trees...flower petal falls
misty morning traffic noise
torn up to
expel wanton...momentary
desire
angst...want...suffice with
watching said flower petals
turn...feed the grass
existence... measured by
lives of trees
who
saw things before me
after me
along side me
that traffic
goes back and forth
up down
the highway...to nowhere

INSPIRATION II

When I am still
before I talk
to the page
it talks to me
tell me it
says
why are you sad
what is it
you want
or need to
say
It has been this
way, now
for almost a year
before
I could never
hear it
out of anger
out of fear
Insane behavior
drugs
crime
loud motor dominance
or facing pay day
disasters, that never seemed to go away
now I still worry
but am very clear
bout what I can
manage plus

even more aware
of what is helpless hopeless tragic beyond words
only prayers, that
are not wishes or dreams
again when I am still
I know
the feeling very well
the paper
never ever
tells me
go to hell

In the times looking back, and what it was ADHD, PTSD, I really think, as I have said before, some fault in my wires from birth. I have embellished and been an exaggerator, mostly just to want to fit and be a part of. That now is not a big deal, due to a lot of years facing my own failure and not the failures of others. I take this now to add to, or end this, with a positive spin and slant that for a lot of years my dwell in the lies and embellishments to make myself either look bigger or more adept at being okay in my own skin. That too has ended, with some rather drastic looks into what and where the times went, down but not out. At 60 years old, I came to Florida to, I thought, change my bad habits and end the lies and the discomfort they bring. It took 10 years of really trying to get honest, but I cannot un-do some of the distorted facts about where and when I did change things to make me appear different than I really was. Now? Full acceptance and tolerance of my own shortcomings and reasons why I need so much attention or crave it, like that whole social media thing where I present myself in bigger frame and smaller honest say about sadness and sorrow. What to write what not to, what to say what not to, even what to think or have rolling around between the ears. It all now needs to somehow end, in what this effort and time was about. Is any one life, anyone's life, more important or more, let's just say, colorful than others? It took me a lot of years to learn that, somehow, I seem to favor being outcast and punished by myself for my own failings. To have now a better sense of how or what to say, about people places and things. It took some sort of repetitive hearing about how many of my fellows in recovery face that same esteem problem and that never fitting in part, too. I have a few really bad weeks, due to some of my, just like I said, partial honest and try to appear bigger smarter faster and more than just the bones and skin that I am.

The last 10 years or so, stable, even if somehow just getting by, was plenty; not falling all over myself with regret and sorrow. Yeah, as I read this over, there was plenty of guilt and shame and being humiliated by my overreaching and thinking that no one really cares. Entertainment? Distractions? The idea that it all only matters to a few, and, by the way, they are both in your life and part of what that part of love really is. It does really occur to me, my mornings when I sit and watch the light change from pre-dawn to the bright light of that sun come over the next-door roof. I revel in it, I really do, learning how to just fucking sit still, not fuss fester or go on with the internal noise. Yeah, that and having had some minor wins about what has been said about my poetry.

More? I really do not know, other than when I can call out to and know who I call is both there for me and part of me.

It has come to the time to wrap this up, with the deep idea my failings were not failing, they were lessons, and even if I did learn the hard way, it all comes out to living better days. I have got all this written, and of the now, life is really good. I've got good friends a good dog a nice house and yard...my energy is not anything like it was. I do, however, know now how to not stumble over my own feet and be in places that are only going to lead me back to the dark side. I've got that good dog, and she and I really enjoy each other. You get a choice every day, to make a good day or wallow in your own confusion and sorrows. I am not about that no more.

I never thought I would live this long, be an old man. Parts of it I relish and some of it is hard to face up to. I do not have anything like the energy I used to, or the real sexual or emotional desire about love and women. Up till 40, all this come out on the pages when I did change the way I acted that led me to change my thinking. I have such a deep gratitude to both AA and CA for the mentors and life-change people who took time with me, to teach me about acting and thinking. I have had this sort of, I think, mixed up set of wires in my internal being, where wrong is just a theory and right is, too. I know way better about that now. This life here with this nice house the best dog alive and some real friends both here and online who are very very dear to me. I have done months of yard work, make the place look like someone really cares and I do. I owe it to those who got me out of my own way, and taught me how *To Be This Man*. My first, in fact, published poems in a book with that title, a memorial collection to Walter Pavich, Swan Scythe Press, with now 13 poetry books out and well reviewed. I think this one has to be better tighter and more fluid than my other memoir *Dear Miss B*. Only how good you feel, how hard you try counts not what you wish would happen.

Yeah, the end parts, the when you become teachable teachers appear, both as friends lovers or out of some place different or similar to yours. Judith Jones who we knew a lot of the same people and lived in the same areas of both NYC and the Bay area in California. She came to visit me here in Florida, and the best cooking and really good to learn from and I even got to teach her how to cast a spinning reel. Yeah, to now we talk just about daily on the phone, her years as a therapist, explaining to me about being your own victim of stuff you did not cause or was somehow part of that broken childhood, things so many of us have lived through. How much I have been helped told taught and learn some on my own to both tolerate and accept things that are not even part of how I act or feel, not judging or argue with any one about some opinion.

It somehow would not be complete without the mention of some names and some, way more than just in passing, people from the ones now still in my life like Roni Hoffman, who I have known since we were both teen age kids in Brooklyn; Susan Andrews, who I know from '68 and we had babies the same year, we would take them to the park on Cortland St and talk, we are online buddies now, she and her husband Buddy did come down and visit me only to add strength to our ongoing relationship; Christina Quinn who lived here almost a year with me and died, that I keep all her paintings on my walls as memory eternal; Linda Post, who I loved from the minute I met her, till when she died too, I was I think in a week long grief that healed itself by the times we did have; Larry and Andrea both of them go back to the '60s too, both of them were big encourage me to write, and be better about my life. The others that are gone, some of them criminals and dope dealers that I am better off now without. To my too much online looking for likes and accolades when my real task is to tell those stories and let this be an essay for recovery and when you get to the bottom of the hole stop digging ...lifted up, I was, and all the men at Loyola and the women like Karen Miller who took me aside and gave me the upshot of being way less about what happened and way more about what you gonna do now. My dear Corina who has helped me make this house a garden spot, and Steve and Becky who bought this house for me, to live in till I die. My daughter Mary, and her love that has never left me, even when I was way less lovable.

I do not know who to include now or not, but anyone who reads this book and knows me knows when and how I care about them...I have not got the idea about a formal end spot, or a list of names places and things. My doctor Kerri, who has taken the best care of me I can say. To the daily bomb in the news and the crazy of now, it can only down me if I let it, and I try all I can not to. Steve and Kris, who are my best advisors and teachers of better writing and ever onward. That my dog, Murphy Quinn, and the life I have now, no matter about money or fame or any of that... What has been planted in my yard will outlive me, yet the care of it is a big part of the care of me. To the now, not all the then, in passing or in jail or in places I might've been better off not going. Leave me here now with, one more time, "If I could an did move on from dumb drunk stoned and stupid you can too." I would love to have Judith come back sometime and teach me some better ways to cook for myself. Care and safety unto length of days, in 2023 heading into 77 years now of one day every day, only now I use the days to be a better man any way I can. What next? Some short stories and more poems, as I will write the best I can till I cannot write any more. I leave now to tell my granddaughter Lillian, "Ya paw paw did the best he could once he got out his own way and learn how to live without anger hate fear or doing damage to anyone and more no more damage to me."

The End Spot

Just before this book goes to print, I must with both a glad and heavy heart mention some names and even some parts of this book I on purpose left out

Steve Gillis	George Jones
Judith Jones	Guy Gavino
Carol S Albanese	Chris Zets
Mary E Albanese	Bill Saunders
Nancy Anello	Larry and Andrea
Kaye Harris	Joe Kara
Alicia Young	Michael Shaver
Carter Monroe	Michael Ivory
Erik Tarlof	David Olin
Seb Dobinsky	Charles Saunders
Gabino Iglesias	Kara Frosh
Roni Hoffman	Mary C Albanese
Donna Lee Phillips	Susanne Sigafoos
Corina Peloni	Dawn Taggblom
Jack St Clair	Judy Bates

and a few other in person and online pals o mine still alive and kicking...AND

FOR THE PASSED ON

Maddy Madison   Sweet William
Spain   Mike Tobin
Linda Post   Nick Torelli
 both my parents and my   Ira Miller
brothers   Giles Yee
  Christina Quinn   Irwin Wiesbrot
  Bruce B   Henry Comato
  Ted Berrigan

all still linger with me in one way or another
Then listed it say takes a village to raise a child it takes a whole collection of support care and encouragement to write a book.

There were some other Sweet William and Linda Post stories I did not tell, so because some of them were hard to face and some of them would go on in me forever. Every time I sit down to write I have what I like to call an invisible telephone that I hear voices on telling me from both long ago and now, write, you were born to tell stories so tell them. Do not ever fall back into dark places and sorrow. Soon enough we all die and if my dad ever really taught me anything it was to be sorry before not after...

Why did I choose an address for a title? A two story wooden home built in 1919 on top of a hill with a full vista view of most of San Francisco. Noe Valley across with the tip of Diamond Heights, then when the fog rolls in the city sort of closes off, to the rest of that view. It really is about time and place in a lot of ways, I might've lost most all my innocence in Vietnam, but when I did get to move into that home, and the next year my daughter would be born and spend the first 4 or 5 years of her life there, it was maybe not innocent but it was fully hopeful, we had it so good. There was a bare dirt-floor back room that in the last time I would see my father, Patty Keen and I fixed it all up and he stayed with us for about two weeks. I did take him all over to meet people and had two nice dinner parties there, where he met Susan Andrews and her then husband Raymond, who was a history teacher, and him and Pop did go on. Raymond was amazed at Patsy's knowing of both history and the meaning of. I see myself now as when I was 22 and, given the times, there was more things possible than not. To where I did not see coming my own complete downfall and the last few months I lived there alone, with only a motorcycle and a VW bus. All the good wood early stuff was gone; Patty sold it all to move her and Mary out and away from me, even if I had not got then as bad as I would, my self-center and self-will run riot was too much for her to bear. I am on good terms with her and my daughter now, as recovery proves the life ya have and the things you do now are more of import than as Joyce called THE STILL DARK PAST.

My amends been made and I have moved on to not be my own enemy or by default a stumble bum or taker. I want to be seen as a giver and good man. If ya read this whole book and ya either like it or learn something bout yr own life I am grateful.